The

THE BEATLES

First published in Great Britain 2003 by
Pocket Essentials, P O Box 394, Harpenden, Herts, AL5 1XJ, UK

Distributed in the USA by Trafalgar Square Publishing,
PO Box 257, Howe Hill Road, North Pomfret, Vermont 05053

A CIP catalogue record for this book is available from the British Library.

ISBN 1-904048-19-6

2 4 6 8 10 9 7 5 3 1

Book typeset by Wordsmith Solutions Ltd
Printed and bound by Cox & Wyman

Dedication

Acknowledgements

Thanks to Ion Mills and Paul Duncan for the pages to fill. Big thanks to Andy and Cora for not being scared of the new sounds and finally to Catherine for the eyes, ears, heart and red pen.

CONTENTS

Introduction: It Was Forty Years Ago Today...

The thing about The Beatles is that here we are with this Pocket Essential publication, celebrating the 40th anniversary of the release of their first album *Please Please Me*, which was released on Friday 22nd March 1963, and globally it could be argued that they are now more popular than ever. A couple of Christmases ago, EMI put together all of the group's number one singles on a compilation, came up with the innovative title of '*1*' and it became the of the fastest selling albums of all time, moving over 23.5 million records in a matter of a month. It has now sold in excess of a phenomenal 35 million copies!

I'm not sure that there are too many people around who don't know The Beatles' story; about how George Harrison, John Lennon, Ringo Starr and Paul McCartney got together, met Brain Epstein and went on to fame and fortune. It's been well documented in hundreds of books over the ensuing 40 years. So the intention here is not to dwell much on that side of things; instead we would like to concentrate on the official recorded works of their short career. On top of which, we'd like to try and shed some light on some of the reasons for their incredible success.

Looking back, it's very easy to say that The Beatles were a megagroup, the biggest and most popular group that the world has ever known. They broke numerous performance records and set standards, commercially and musically speaking, which I believe will never be bettered. But their success wasn't an accident. The important thing in all of this wasn't that they had so many hits because they were a big group; the reason they had so many hits was simply because they had great songs.

I find it incredible that you could go out on the street and walk up to a stranger and mention a song title, any one of their 208 songs, and nine times out of ten the stranger would be able to make a passable stab at singing the melody. We're not just talking about the twenty-two official singles here, or even their B-sides. Try it at your place of work or in the pub or at a dinner party. Even simpler than that, take a look at the list of their recorded titles at the back and see how many of them you can remember and/or sing.

Let's take a chronological trip through the fantastic adventure of The Beatles using their singles and albums as islands along the way and maybe with a few prompts here and there on the various songs, I might even be able to help you to remember some of the tunes in question. Without further ado...

1: Come Together

First there was John - John Winston Lennon. Born in Liverpool October 9th 1940. John, an only child, was brought up by his Aunt Mary - 'Mimi' - and Uncle George Smith because his dad was away at sea and his mother, Julia, was living with another man. His Uncle George died in 1955. John attended Quarry Bank Grammar School; he loved books, writing stories and drawing. Julia apparently could play anything with strings and taught John ukulele chords. Thanks to the skiffle craze sweeping the country in 1956 - led in no small way by Lonnie Donegan and his number one single *Rock Island Line* - John Lennon formed a skiffle group called The Quarrymen with his mates from Quarry Bank School. The following year, on 6th July 1957, the Quarrymen were performing at Woolton Parish Church Fete, where a young man called Paul McCartney was in the audience. Following the Quarrymen's second set John Lennon was introduced to Paul McCartney by a mutual friend, Ivan Vaughan. John's mother was very tragically killed, knocked down by a motorcar just outside her house, a few months before John's eighteenth birthday in 1958.

Paul James McCartney was born in Liverpool on 18th June 1942 to Mary and James McCartney. He had a younger brother, Michael. His mother died of breast cancer in 1956. Paul, influenced by his father, who had once led a local jazz band, took up music and by the time he met John he was able to play a little. It was his ability to teach John some chords and the fact that he knew and could write down the lyrics to some of John's favourite songs that encouraged John to invite Paul to join The Quarrymen. Paul McCartney attended Liverpool Institute and on his daily trip to this learning establishment, on the number 86 bus, he would frequently meet up with fellow pupil and musician George Harrison.

George Harrison was born on 25th February 1943, the fourth child of Louise and Harold Harrison. George had two brothers and one sister. By the time George met Paul, although a year younger, he was a veteran of two groups - The Rebels and The Les Stewart Quartet. George first heard the Quarrymen in early 1958 and he joined their ever-changing line-up in August 1959.

In January 1960 the Quarrymen, consisting of John, Paul and George with John's friend Stuart Sutcliffe on bass, became the Beatals. They changed their name to the Silver Beetles, with drummer Tommy Moore, but by August of that year Tommy Moore was gone and they were off to play a residency in Hamburg as The Beatles with Pete Best as the drummer.

The Hamburg residency was a baptism of fire. There was music, alcohol, pills and sex. They would play for several hours each night, and encouraged by the club owner continually shouting 'Mach Schau' at them, they gradually became very tight. They had the ability to start a song together, keep in time for the duration and then finish it together. No amount of rehearsal can teach you to be tight; it's an intuitive thing that happens when musicians know each other very well. By the time they returned home they were, musically speaking, one of the best of the 300 or so groups playing around Liverpool at that time.

Stuart Sutcliffe fell in love with the stylish Hamburg student and photographer Astrid Kirchherr and following The Beatles' second visit to Germany he remained in Hamburg to continue studying his first love, art. Stuart died tragically in Astrid's arms from cerebral paralysis on 10th April 1962. He was John's best friend and was the first Beatle, inspired and styled by Astrid, to have the Beatle haircut, wear the black leather suit and the velvet Cardin suits.

Astrid's early Hamburg photo sessions with The Beatles clearly show the band evolving from a bunch of Liverpool scruffs into a band with an image. They looked like family, more brothers than fellow musicians. The Beatles couldn't help but notice that they were starting to look as though they belonged and, more importantly, that they belonged together. The leather suits and the haircuts helped to cultivate this look but there was more: the long hours together on stage each night; living in each other's pockets; making sure they gave each other as good as they got; their pain; their mutual love of American music; but probably above all, it was the confidence they were starting to feel and share that set them apart from other bands.

In May 1961, The Beatles visited the recording studios for the first time. They were the backing band for Tony Sheridan and recorded *My Bonnie*, which was released as a single in June 1961 under the name Tony Sheridan and the Beat Brothers. The brief change of name occurred because the producer of the sessions, Bert Kaempfert, decided that 'The Beatles' sounded like the German word for penis. During this first recording session The Beatles also recorded *Cry For A Shadow,* a George Harrison-composed instrumental, which earns the distinction of being the first Beatle original to appear on an album (Tony Sheridan's German release of *My Bonnie* in June 1962). Towards the end of the summer of 1961, back in

Liverpool, a local businessman, encouraged by people coming into the record department of his shop and requesting *My Bonnie* and the reports he was reading about The Beatles in the local music paper, *Mersey Beat*, went to see them in the Cavern Club. This local businessman was none other than Brian Epstein, and he visited the Cavern at lunchtime on 9th Nov 1961. He loved the performance and visited the band briefly in the dressing room. A month later he returned again to the Cavern for The Beatles but this time he left a message with George that he'd like them all to come and meet him at his office, NEMS.

Brain Samuel Epstein was born on 19th Nov 1934 to Harry and Queenie Epstein. He had one brother, Clive, who was twenty-two months younger. Brian went to work in the family business in 1950. At 18 years of age he was conscripted for National Service. He was discharged after ten months and returned to the family business. In 1956, when he was 22, influenced by a lot of the new friends he was meeting at the Playhouse Theatre, he passed the audition to study at RADA (Royal Academy of Dramatic Arts). He did not complete the course and returned to the family business in 1957 to run the record department in his father's newly opened NEMS store in Great Charlotte Street. This was such a success that they opened another branch in Whitechapel and it was into this store that the first known Beatles fan, Raymond Jones, walked one morning and placed an order for *My Bonnie*. Numerous members of the nearby Cavern Club had been requesting this record at NEMS but it was only Raymond Jones' name that was entered into the order book and into history.

The first meeting between Brian Epstein and The Beatles was set for 4.30pm on Wednesday 3rd December 1961, at NEMS. The fastidious Brian Epstein was annoyed that The Beatles were all late, especially Paul who was, according to the others, luxuriating in the bath.

'Oh he's very late,' Brian said just before 5.00pm.

'Yes, but he'll be very clean,' George replied with the razor-sharp tongue that was fast becoming part of The Beatles' magic.

Brian met John, Paul, George and Pete again on December 10th and it was agreed that he would become their manager. According to the initial contract, he would receive 10% of any income up to £1500 per year. (Equivalent of £18,000, in 2003. The rough rule of thumb is to multiply all 1960s pound values by twelve to get the 2003 equivalent) and 15% of everything thereafter. By 1962 his commission was increased to 25%. He would also advise them on clothes, makeup, presentation and their act.

The Beatles' famous trademark low bow at the end of their performances was a Brian Epstein idea.

When Brian Epstein met The Beatles they were rough diamonds. They smoked, chewed gum, swore on stage and were still wearing their leather gear. Brian cleaned up the act and dressed them in identical Mohair suits, made by his tailor, Beno Dorn. Brian Epstein added the professional touches that set them apart from the rest of the Liverpool groups. The Beatles, for their part, worked tirelessly and their regular spots at the Cavern Club showed *just* how tight they'd become through the many hours of playing in Hamburg. The Beatles were causing pandemonium at the Cavern, with the audience egging the band on to even greater heights. The early seeds of Beatlemania were being sown!

Brian Epstein was new to the management side of the music business but he wasn't scared of asking questions, taking advice and using his record contacts from the retail side to fix up meeting with the various record companies. Initially the London record companies treated him and The Beatles abysmally, but these were the days when England ended just north of Watford. Time after time he would return on the London-Liverpool train with his tail between his legs, having been rejected by the likes of Decca, EMI or Pye. But any misgivings or doubts he experienced would have disappeared as he witnessed the hysteria The Beatles were causing at any one of their 292 Cavern appearances. To keep the home fires burning at the beginning of January 1962, they were voted Liverpool's top band in *Mersey Beat*.

This period of rejection (by the London record companies) lasted for over a year and the relationship between band and manager must have been pretty fragile at times. Brian though was totally committed to The Beatles and his ability to get back up and dust himself off after the numerous rejections led him on May 8th 1962 to yet another meeting in London with yet another London record company; this time it was Parlophone Records' boss, George Martin. Parlophone was a wing – a left wing would be a good description – of EMI Records who had also already turned Brian down.

George Martin was born in London in 1926. He joined the Air Force at the age of 17 and when he was 21 (1937) he joined the Guildhall School of Music, London, to train as a classical musician. He is the epitome of the perfect English Gentleman: cultured, sophisticated, well mannered and well spoken. He left the Guildhall to work in the BBC Music Library and in 1950 went to work as assistant to the head of Parlophone. In 1955 he was promoted (on the retirement of his boss) to the head of Parlophone. Parlophone was famous for such artists as Peter Sellers, Matt Monro, Beyond the Fringe, The Temperance Seven, and The Goons.

It's odd how two people can attend the same meeting, be involved in the same conversation, and yet... come away with opposing views. Brian Epstein thought the meeting had gone perfectly and, even though he'd secured only an audition in EMI's London studios for the band, he sent the boys and *Mersey Beat* a telegram saying, essentially, that the band had a *confirmed* recording contract with Parlophone. George Martin, for his part, has been quoted as saying that he didn't think that the Decca (rejection) Tapes that Brian played him were any good but he felt sorry for Brian because he knew The Beatles' personable manager had been turned down by nearly everyone in town, and so the big-hearted record company boss couldn't find a way to say no to the manager on the spot. The audition he offered was simply as a stopgap.

However, the end result was exactly the same, because The Beatles had their much sought after, and needed, audition and on 6th June 1962 they visited Abbey Road Studios, London NW1 for the first time. These four rather thin and strange looking Liverpudlians - with their mate, driver and helper Neil Aspinall - unpacked their rickety gear from the back of their clapped out white van. The band recorded *Besame Mucho* – a Valazquez/ Shaftel song, which was a hit for Mario Lanza and the Coasters, among others - and three McCartney & Lennon (as they were then credited) compositions, *Love Me Do*, *P.S. I Love You* and *Ask Me Why*. The session went quite well, the studio staff was averagely impressed by the original songs. At the end of the session, George Martin gave John, Paul, George and Pete a long lecture on their equipment and how they'd need to improve it if they wanted to become recording artists. The Beatles remained silent for the lecture and at the end of it George Martin asked them if there was anything they'd like to pass comment on. They looked at each nervously and shuffled around for a few embarrassing seconds until George Harrison said, 'Yeah, I don't like your tie!' This broke the ice; I feel it represented the beginning of the bonding between the most famous and successful group and producer team that the world has ever known. That one little remark and its reaction showed that The Beatles in general, and George Harrison in particular, while they were respectful of men in suits, were neither in awe of them or subservient to them. From George Martin's point of view his reaction showed that he was not a stiff suit and, apparently, the following twenty minutes were a total hoot with everyone relaxed and enjoying the warmth and humour of their Northern visitors. It was quite possible that this interaction which was responsible for The Beatles being offered their first, albeit abysmal, recording contract.

They were signed to a one-year contract during which they would record four songs, and they would receive one old penny (2.4 old pence equal 1 new pence) per double sided single. Parlophone would have an option to extend the first year by an additional four single year periods if they so desired. Not a great deal as deals were soon to become but Brian Epstein knew that one of the big secrets of the music business was never to waste time by haggling over money until there's money to be haggled over. With their recording contract The Beatles now had a chance to get their infectious music out beyond the Liverpool City limits.

But not before one final piece of the jigsaw was to be replaced. Although Pete Best fitted as *part* of the puzzle, he did not work well inside the big picture, and he was sacked. His replacement was Ringo Starr; but the first picture of Ringo, complete with his Tony Curtis DA and beard while John, Paul and George sported their Astrid inspired look, could hardly have been the perfectly formed jigsaw puzzle either!

Ringo Starr was born Richard Starkey on 7th July 1940 to Elsie and Richard Starkey. His parents divorced in 1943. Richard was plagued with various illnesses – he was in hospital for several months when he was six, with a ruptured appendix and complications, and between the ages of thirteen and fifteen, with chronic pleurisy - consequently his education suffered. He worked as a messenger for British Rail, a barman on the New Brighton Ferry and as a trainee joiner. With some of his workmates he formed a skiffle group in 1957, playing drums on a second-hand kit his stepfather bought him. He played in various groups before joining Rory Storm & The Hurricanes. Rory Storm, a larger than life showman, renamed Richard Ringo Starr, and during the Hurricanes' performances, Ringo would have a solo spot known as Ringo's Starrtime and he would sing *Boys* and *You're Sixteen*. The Hurricanes were 'big in Hamburg' and during the winter of 1960 The Beatles supported them in the German city. In August 1962 Ringo received his invitation to join The Beatles.

2: The First Two Singles:
Love Me Do & Please Please Me

During John, Paul, George & Ringo's first proper recording session at Abbey Road, on Tuesday 6th September 1962, they recorded *Love Me Do* and *How Do You Do It*. The latter was a Mitch Murray & Barry Mason song, which George Martin had recommended to The Beatles. Although they recorded the song for their producer they made it clear to him they only wanted to record their own material. This was a major statement for a newly signed band to make. In the sixties there were songwriters and then there were performers and very rarely would they be one and the same. But both parties were to be proven right. The Beatles would go on to incredible success with their self-penned songs and George Martin recorded *How Do You Do It* with Gerry And The Pacemakers, whose version topped the charts for four weeks.

The Beatles returned to the studio the following week and re-recorded *Love Me Do,* this time with a session musician Andy White on drums and Ringo on Tambourine. Ringo probably thought they were about to do a Pete Best on him. Both versions of *Love Me Do* are in circulation and the easiest way to tell them apart is the one without the tambourine is the Ringo version and the one with the tambourine is the Alan White version. They also recorded *P.S. I Love You* and took a stab at recording *Please Please Me* - both with Ringo drumming.

After two long recording sessions they had their debut single *Love Me Do,* backed with *P.S. I Love You,* in the can and it was released on Friday 5th Oct 1962 on Parlophone Records (R 4949). It peaked at number 17 in the UK that December with most of the copies apparently being bought in the Liverpool area and the majority of those in one particular chain of shops. The week that *Love Me Do* reached number 17, Elvis Presley was number 1 with *Return To Sender*. The full chart read:

1.	Elvis Presley	Return to Sender
2.	Cliff Richard	Next Time
3.	The Shadows	Dance On!
4.	Duane Eddy	Dance With The Guitar Man
5.	Frank Ifield	Lovesick Blues
6.	Brenda Lee	Rocking Around the Christmas Tree

7. Rolf Harris	Sun Arise
8. The Tornados	Telstar
9. Susan Maughan	Bobby's Girl
10.Chris Montez	Let's Dance
11.Stan Getz & Charlie Byrd	Desafinado
12.Del Shannon	Swiss Maid
13.Ray Charles	Your Cheating Heart
14.Marty Robbins	Devil Woman
15.Joe Brown	It Only Took A Minute
16.Pat Boone	The Main Attraction
17. The Beatles	Love Me Do
18.Hank Lockin	We're Going Fishing
19.Bobby Vee	A Forever Kind Of Love
20.Sinatra & Davis Jr.	Me And My Shadow

I list the top twenty here so that you can consider what the musical climate was like when The Beatles arrived on the scene. Other names in that week's top fifty were Joe Loss, The Springfields, The Four Seasons, The Crystals, Chubby Checker, Patsy Cline, Nat King Cole, the Everly Brothers, Little Eva and Ella Fitzgerald, with her own version of *Desafinado*. Adam Faith at number 23 and Bernard Cribbins at 35 were the only other Parlophone Records' artists who were in the charts that week.

The Beatles were the first leaderless group. Marketing-wise, George Martin probably had to consider the possibility of leading with the cute Paul or the strong personality of John to emulate the likes of Cliff and the Shadows or Elvis and The Jordanaires, but he stuck with The Beatles' one-for-all-and-all-for-one approach. In hindsight it's easy to say that he, and they, were right to stick to their guns, but at the same time you have to recognise that the few media opportunities available were set up for the Cliffs, the Elvises, the Pats, The Brendas, The Billys and the Bobbies and so on.

We are talking about a time when the old show business school had such a tight grasp on the music scene that they nearly strangled it. The Beatles had their magic, their music, their fanatical fans and the unwavering belief of their manager that he was lucky enough to be managing a group of musicians who were the best (including Elvis) and were going to be the biggest.

One of the main qualities of Brian and his charges was that they all realised that the main event was not just securing a record deal. Apart from anything else, Parlophone was considered a comedy eclectic label. The label's other releases at the time of *Love Me Do* were The King Brothers, Johnny Angel, Nicky Hilton, Shane Fenton & the Fentones (Shane would eventually shed his Fentones for a bit of Stardust), James Brown & The Famous Flames, The Temperance Seven, Matt Monro, Houston Wells and The Marksmen, Ken Jones and His Orchestra, Jill Graham; the aforementioned Adam Faith and Bernard Cribbins were the only other label mates in the charts with The Beatles. No, manager and band knew that securing a record was only the first step. Now the real work was about to begin.

During this period The Beatles and Brian Epstein invented the template for a movement that was to follow thirteen years later, namely the Punks. Out of necessity they made a business inside the old fashioned traditional business. Their attitude was, 'Just because you won't let us play and sell our music inside your show business system, doesn't mean we're going to go away, lay down and die.'

The Beatles and the Punks found their own places to play, they built their own circuit, they found their own media outlets, and they found their own record labels. In The Beatles' case they signed with a comedy label. In the Punks' day they had their very own independent labels, mainly Stiff Records. But it really didn't matter who put the records out because they (Beatles and Punks) had an eager, waiting audience. These eager audiences were soon buying records in such quantities that it wasn't long before the 'official' music business embraced The Beatles (in 1965) and the Punks (in 1978) as their own.

Unlike the Punks though, The Beatles kept their autonomy; in fact, they grew even more independent in the later stages of their career, forming Apple Records, a company which to this day is the keeper and fan of the Beatle flame, with their chum Neil Aspinall loyally at the helm.

The Beatles played and played, onwards and outwards in ever increasing circles from Liverpool. It's not only that they were working every day; most days they were doing two shows plus, possibly, a television or radio appearance or even both for good measure. Now and again, as on Monday 26th November 1962, they'd even nip down to London to the Abbey Road studios for a quick recording session.

The Beatles had already tried a pass at *Please Please Me*. In its original form it was more of a Roy Orbison-type big ballad. George Martin thought the song had potential but detested the treatment. The Beatles changed the arrangement by making it more up-tempo and adding a harmonica. Ringo's work on the track was enough to allow him to reclaim the drum seat *permanently*. At the same session The Beatles successfully recorded *Ask Me Why* - another McCartney/Lennon tune - which was released as the B-side to *Please Please Me* on Friday 11th Jan 1963.

George Martin declared over the studio intercom, 'You've just made your first number one.' George Martin's bold prediction was proven correct six short but very busy weeks later.

Please Please Me made the number one spot in the charts compiled by *The New Musical Express* and *Melody Maker* and *Disc,* while the charts compiled by *The Record Retailer* listed them at number two. The *Record Retailer* chart was *the* official industry chart - although the *NME* was the chart used by the weekly *Top Of The Pops* television show. Whatever way you looked at it, The Beatles had their first UK smash hit single.

They returned to the studios on Monday 11th Feb and in one amazing ten-hour session - costing all of £400 - they recorded a further ten songs, which along with the A and B-sides of the first two singles would make up their first long playing album. What's even more amazing about this session is that it happened at all. The Beatles had been working, day-in and day-out and night-in and night-out, since 1960, playing everywhere they could. They did every radio session, every photo session and every television slot that was offered. With *Please Please Me* being the smash hit that it was, the industry demanded that they have a long player (album) in the shops at the earliest moment to cash in on the success. So George Martin took their next available day (Monday 11th Feb 1963) and scheduled it as a recording day.

One of the hardest winters in years and all of the live work had taken its toll on the group, particularly John who was suffering from a very sore throat. Helped by a non-stop supply of tea, throat lozenges and (absurdly) cigarettes, they got through their session, making a classic debut album in the process.

At this point the music of Liverpool, in the form of The Beatles, was being heard nationwide. They appeared on *Thank Your Lucky Stars*, a television show with high viewing figures. They appeared on their first package tour – headlined by teenage singing sensation Helen Shapiro. John Lennon and Paul McCartney were also starting to attract attention as songwriters outside of the Beatle camp, penning songs for Helen Shapiro (*Misery,* which her producer rejected but was later picked up and recorded by Kenny Lynch) and *I'll Be On My Way* for Billy J Kramer, who was coincidently also managed by Brian Epstein. A second package tour with Chris Montez and Tommy Roe followed. As was the case with the Helen Sha-

17

piro, Brian Epstein had modestly not booked The Beatles as the headline group but, as was also the case with their first package tour, the audience demanded The Beatles and so the Fabs closed the shows from the second night onwards.

Another landmark in their career was that on Monday 4th March 1963 they achieved their first £100 booking. It was in the Plaza Ballroom in St Helens. The following day at 2.30 pm they were in Abbey Road Studios recording the two tracks which were to become their third single, *From Me To You* and *Thank You Girl*.

3: The First Album: *Please Please Me.*

Please Please Me the album was released on Parlophone Records (PCS 3042) on 22nd March 1963. The majority of the songs were taken from The Beatles' then current live set and the original idea for it had been to record it as a live album in the Cavern. It had a working title of *Off The Beatle Track*. Perhaps EMI were still unsure of the potential of their new charges and wanted to find a quick economic way of recording a cash in on the success of the hit single. Whatever the reason, the Cavern approach was dropped and George Martin and the group had one day in Abbey Road Studios to complete work on their first long player.

The sleeve advised us that we were about to enjoy '*Please Please Me*, with *Love Me Do* and 10 other titles.' The photograph on the cover was taken by Angus McBean at the EMI Building in Manchester Square in the West End of London. The sleeve shows four fresh-faced Scousers smiling down at you. Ringo their most recent recruit was still to acquire their trademark Beatle haircut.

The album featured eight songs credited to McCartney and Lennon although their publicist, Tony Barrow, in his sleeve notes refers to them as Lennon and McCartney songs. The remaining six songs were covers The Beatles had been performing on stage. Paul McCartney has gone on record as saying that the main reason he and John started writing so many song was because they'd be sitting in their dressing waiting to go on stage and they'd hear the support group perform some of the covers they were just about to do themselves. If that's true then it means that the most successful songwriting partnership in the world was formed just because The Beatles wanted to perform songs no one else was doing.

The standout track on that first album was the opening cut, *I Saw Her Standing There*. Up until the 11th February recording date, it was still being referred to as *Just Seventeen*. It's a classic throat-grabbing, toe-tapping, timeless, rock song, which immediately appeared in the set lists of most of the other groups playing around the Merseyside at that time. I've never been too hung up about if a song was a John song or a Paul song. To me they're all Beatle songs if The Beatles recorded them. However for those who like to know these things, the general rule was if John sings lead it's a John song and if Paul sings lead it's a Paul song and if George sang lead it was a George song (unless of course John and Paul wrote it for their favourite lead guitarist) and if Ringo sang lead it was a Lennon &

McCartney song and if Brian Epstein sang lead it was because he'd just caught a glimpse of the publishing royalties.

The second song on *Misery* shows exactly how wonderful the gift had been that Helen Shapiro's producer had turned down. Although, for me, the hidden gem on the record is *There's A Place*. This more than most of the songs hinted at what Lennon & McCartney were capable of. Before *There's A Place* the songs were great, songs that wouldn't have been out of place in any of the big musicals, but *There's A Place* was introspective and at the time it was a very brave song for the mop tops to be recording. With *Do You Want To Know A Secret* Paul showed he was probably the most versatile of The Beatles by his ability to croon with the best, and still had the little round things necessary to deliver *I Saw Her Standing There* with the best of the rockers.

The final track, *Twist and Shout,* hits you over the head just as effectively as the opening track. The song had already been recorded by The Top Notes and was a US hit in 1962 for The Isley Brothers; it was written by Bert Russell (real name Bern Berns) and Phil Medley. The song had been recorded as an afterthought because at the end of the sessions, George Martin thought they needed one more song to finish off the album. At which point John's voice was all but shot, but he gave his best and although they took two passes at the song, the one that you hear on the record today is their first take and John's evident enthusiasm and total recall of their Hamburg nights obviously took its toll because for the next couple of shows The Beatles had to perform as a trio; John's cold and sore throat had caught up with him and he was ordered to bed.

I still find it hard to believe that The Beatles - John in particular - were capable of such high standards after a long day in the studio. The session started at 10.00 am and was completed at 10.45 pm. The Beatles declined their producer's invitation to a lunch break, preferring instead to use the time to rehearse the songs they were scheduled to record in the afternoon. I still get a lump in my throat when I listen to *Twist and Shout.* It's a classic song, but The Beatles in that one take had made it their own, they'd recorded a version that would never be bettered. Just listen to the raw energy, the enthusiasm, and the tightness. Listen to the amazing blend of the voices. It's such an infectious sound and I suppose the main thing it shows about The Beatles in those days was that, apart from anything else, they were a cracking great wee rock band.

The Beatles first album broke into the top ten on 30th March 1963. The full top ten albums were:

1. Cliff Richard & The Shadows.   Summer Holiday
2. Frank Sinatra & Count Basie   Sinatra & Basie
3. Frank Ifield   I'll Remember You
4. Various Artists   All Star Festival
5. Elvis Presley   Girls! Girls! Girls!
6. Buddy Holly   Reminiscing
7. Soundtrack   West Side Story
8. Soundtrack   South Pacific
9. The Beatles   Please Please Me
10. The Shadows   Out of the Shadows

On May 11th 1963 they reached the coveted top slot, displacing Cliff & The Shadows. The Beatles were about to embark on yet another package tour. This time they would headline a bill that also included Roy Orbison. On top of which the BBC gave them a weekly radio show, Pop Go The Beatles, which was just incredible, really, for a group who less than a year before didn't even have a recording contract!

4: Beatlemania: *She Loves You* &
I Want to Hold Your Hand & *With The Beatles*

Their third single, *From Me To You,* was released on Parlophone (R5015) on Thursday 11th April 1963. John and Paul wrote this song on the back of the tour bus on the Helen Shapiro Package Tour. It entered the charts just as *Please Please Me*, the single, was leaving and shot to the number one position, where it remained for several weeks. Simultaneously, over on the album charts, *Please Please Me* was ensconced at the top where it would proudly and securely remain for the next several months.

From Me To You, of all the Beatle singles, is the one that has stood the test of time least well. It's a great single and a good song but I can't help thinking it was a bit of a stopgap. Martin and Epstein had come up with this plan to release a single every three months and two albums a year. Singles tended to hang around the charts for three months and albums for about six months, which probably meant that the reason behind their master plan was that they wanted The Beatles to have a continued presence in the charts.

Overkill? No matter what hype is going on, the public will only buy what it wants to hear and The Beatles, apart from on this one occasion, were always coming up with something completely different. No two songs ever sounded the same. Fans didn't think that they were buying this year's version of last year's hits.

If there was a gap that Epstein and Martin felt needed filling, *From Me To You* certainly filled it and… that's all it did, although it's interesting to note that, unlike the first two singles, it didn't make the first album. Maybe it did serve as a bit of a breather and if that's what it was meant to be it was certainly very effective because The Beatles were about to start on several years of creativity that no other artist would ever come within a million miles of.

Brian Epstein and his charges kept up their onslaught on the UK and Ireland, performing on stages large and small. The Beatles first £250 booking was on May 17th 1963 in the Grosvenor Rooms, Norwich. But all were not that big, some were so small that in the time between first booking the show and the night of the performance, the band had so outgrown the venue that it would have been dangerous to both band and audience to go ahead with them, so Epstein had to buy them out of all such shows. As before, they would intersperse these gigs with quick visits to the studio to record Lennon & McCartney's most recent efforts. And so in this climate came the fourth single *She Loves You* (Parlophone R 5055, August 23rd 1963). It was exactly what the doctor ordered. It was new, it was fresh, it was vibrant, it was infectious… and it could only have been The Beatles. It was their early signature sound. John and Paul co-wrote this song in their hotel room following a gig in the Majestic Ballroom, Newcastle on Wed 26th June 1963.

Five days later they recorded it at Abbey Road with George Martin, who was intrigued by George Harrison's final chord on the song, a major sixth. No, I don't know what it is either but you have to admit that it does sound very pleasing. You'd have say, listening to it today, that this was a song *recorded* by George Martin rather than a song *produced* by him. It's a song that clearly benefits performance-wise from their many hours on stage together. It also shows that the group had been subconsciously noting why the classic covers - they were performing in that wee club in Hamburg's Reaperbaun – were in fact classic and why they went down as well with the audience as they did. It also shows that the club owner continually screaming 'Mach Schau' (make show) at them had made a lasting impression. This song is very audience-friendly, and every artist The Beatles covered and praised would have been happy to put their name to this dance floor filler.

To many people – even today – *She Loves You* is The Beatles at their best. The single was released on 23rd August 1963 – the same week that *Please Please Me* the album was enjoying its fifteenth week at number one in the album charts – and shot straight to number one, where it stayed for four weeks. The single became The Beatles' first million-seller and in fact was the biggest selling single in the UK for about the next decade. The Beatles burst completely into the public consciousness. The press loved the 'Yeah, Yeah, Yeah' phrase and trooped it out at every headline opportunity. By this point the press pack and television crews were starting to follow the Fab Four everywhere.

On Sunday 13th October they performed *She Loves You* and the B-side, *I'll Get You*, on *Sunday Night At The London Palladium*, the prime entertainment television show that had topped the viewing ratings for several years. The following morning the press introduced the word 'Beatlemania' to describe the fans' reaction to the band, in and around the venue. As a result of this performance the single *She Loves You*, which had been hanging around the top three of the singles charts for two months, returned to the coveted number one spot for a further two weeks. This was a feat previously unheard of and I can't think of anyone else who has managed to repeat it.

The second Parlophone album, *With The Beatles* (PMC 1206), was released 22nd November 1963 with a phenomenal advance order of 300,000. It went straight to number one, reaching half a million sales within a matter of weeks. The Beatles had the number one and number two album and the number one and number two single in the UK during the last week of November 1963. Unbelievably, the sales for the album were so strong the *album* entered the singles chart as well, peaking at number eleven and hanging around for a couple of months. The classic cover was an Astrid-influenced shot by Robert Freeman. They'd perfected the mop top image by this stage; they looked magnificent but they played even better. Ringo's work on *She Loves You* was one of the highlights of the track.

With The Beatles offered up another fourteen Beatle gems. As we've already mentioned, in the early 1960s, an album was merely released by the record company to cash in on the success of a single – the single ruled. The accompanying album would have the single plus another nine or ten tracks of little consequence. The Beatles changed all of that. Number one, after the first album, they rarely included any of their singles on their albums but more about that later. Number two, each and every track had to fight for its inclusion on the album. Then they put energy, time and money into their sleeves (dust jackets), first developing the gatefold sleeve and then including the lyrics to the songs on the jacket. The Beatles made the album an accepted art form. The Beatles also never subscribed to having fodder for the B-sides of their singles, on numerous occasions releasing value for money double A-sided singles.

Their recent spate of song writing was not just an isolated burst, but a fine example of what lay ahead. *All I've Got To Do* (with a deeper than normal lyric, a beautiful song) and then *All My Loving* (a classic, it could have been a single, should have been a single) covered by everyone from Count Basie to the Chipmunks. Then we've got the song they polished off in the back of a taxi for the Rolling Stones, *I Wanna Be Your Man*, definitely a sound suited to the maraca driven R'n'B sound the Stones were borrowing, but, at the same time, the song was also suitable for Ringo's lazy vocal style. *Don't Bother Me* was George's debut song writing effort, written for a journalist who kept asking him how his song writing was coming on. *Little Child* was a harmonica-led song. It was interesting that the British were dropping the traditional name for this instrument – the mouth organ – in favour of the more flattering (musically speaking) American title; perhaps the change in name even had something to do with sexual innuendo? *Not A Second Time* was the Lennon & McCartney song that the critic from *The Times* went over the top about. For him it had The Beatles 'thinking simultaneously of harmony and melody, so firmly are the major tonic sevenths and ninths built into their tunes, and the flat sub-mediant key switches, so natural is the Aeolian cadence at the end of *Not a Second Time*.' Aeolian cadence and the flat submediant key changes, was it indeed? And here I was thinking it was just a cracking wee foot-tapping tune! For the remainder of the material on *With The Beatles*, the group continued working their way through their Hamburg set. Here they suc-cessfully nailed these often-played cover versions, none better so than *Money.* Chuck Berry was introduced to a wider UK audience with the Fabs' effective version of *Roll Over Beethoven*. *You Really Got A Hold On Me,* with George Martin playing piano on a Beatles record for the first time, displays an incredible vocal performance from John and Paul, sell-ing you instantly on Smokey Robinson's song as if it were their own.

She Loves You was knocked off the top of the singles charts by a single which immediately broke another record by being the first UK single to have an advance order of ONE MILLION copies! And the name of the artists responsible for this incredible achievement? Why, The Beatles of course, and the song was *I Want To Hold Your Hand* (Parlophone R 5084 Released 29th November 1963).

When The Beatles followed up *She Loves You* with *I Want To Hold Your Hand* – one classic after another – you knew there was something special going on in their camp. Even the Americans sat up and paid atten-tion. Capitol Records had turned down The Beatles' first four singles. One is forgivable, two could maybe be considered a mistake, three (the second consecutive UK number one) was just not on and four was downright insulting! Vee Jay Records released the first two US singles, *Please Please Me* and *From Me To You,* and then they switched to Swan Records for *She Loves You,* which like its two predecessors did nothing; but fol-lowing their initial success, *She Loves You* showed its worth when it was re-released on Capitol and this time it topped the American charts. *Love Me Do* wasn't released until much later and then as part of the Capitol Records deal. George Martin and Brian Epstein showed that they were more forgiving of Capitol than the fans were and kept on knocking on

Capitol's door. The company took to *I Want To Hold Your Hand* and thought it would be perfect for the American market.

A DJ from Washington started to play a copy of *I Want To Hold Your Hand* imported for him by his girlfriend, who was an air hostess. Such was the reaction that Capitol increased the ship-out figure from 200,000 to 1,000,000. One million copies and they hadn't even released The Beatles' previous four singles! The Beatles were playing a long run in the legendary Paris Olympia when they received the news that *I Want To Hold Your Hand* had shot to number one in America and there it remained for seven weeks.

Okay, we have The Beatles, a group of four working-class lads, not embarrassed by their accents, their roots or hard work. They looked different and they looked great with their Beatle mop top haircuts, collarless jackets; Cuban heeled Beatle Boots and polo neck black pullovers. Their look, which had been inspired by Astrid and her friends, had become the fashion copied by all The Beatles' fans.

They could write superb songs.

They could sing well and played together competently as a group.

They had a distinctive, infectious, original sound.

They gave a good interview. They were naturally very funny, a humour which was probably helped rather than hindered by their unique Liverpudlian accents.

They liked each other; they could bicker and argue with the best of them, but they were good friends and respected each other.

The Beatles were truly loved by their audience. They had a lot of time and respect for their audience. They even went as far as answering the fan mail themselves, something unheard of in the entertainment world.

They were huge music fans themselves and had an excellent knowledge of recording artists, particularly the American artists, because of their love of American music.

They loved what they were doing and weren't scared, while on stage, to show they were enjoying their own music.

They benefited from perfect timing.

They had a manager with superior organisational skills, a theatrical leaning, a vision and an unequalled love for his charges.

And then you had America!

America the biggest, most affluent, consumer friendly country in the whole wide world, which had a music industry older and more professional than its British counterparts, an industry which to date had shunned everything British, including the likes of Cliff Richard and Adam Faith.

The Beatles and their manager had registered this and come up with a brave plan, considering that it was concocted when they didn't even have a proper record company to release their records in America. They would go to America *only* when they had a number one single! Not for them the cap in hand! Well, the plan worked beautifully, and now they had their number one single in America. What next?

Luckily enough, Ed Sullivan, the host of the American equivalent of a cross between *Sunday Night At The London Palladium* and *Parkinson,* and probably the most powerful man on American television, just happened to be travelling through London's Heathrow Airport when The Beatles were returning from a successful Swedish visit. Their fans had turned out in their thousands in the hope of catching a glimpse of them. So when Epstein approached Sullivan a few weeks after, the latter was very receptive. The Beatles' manager was looking for far more than a guest spot. Brian Epstein successfully negotiated *three* successive headline appearances on the top rated NBC *Ed Sullivan Show.*

This was every bit as big an achievement as, say, John and Paul sitting down and writing *She Loves You* or *I Want To Hold Your Hand.* Over the years, the myth has been propagated, mostly by envious managers, that Brian Epstein was not a good manager; that he didn't make good deals. Rubbish. Brian Epstein was in uncharted waters. Everyone who'd gone before him had failed. Epstein realised that the secret of doing a successful deal was that first you had to reach an agreement. There was no need to go chasing those extra pennies. In his case, be it with Parlophone Records, television and radio producers, concert promoters, merchandisers, it was important that he made a deal to provide an opportunity which would expose The Beatles and their infectious music to the world. I genuinely believe that was his vision.

And what a vision! The planning of the debut in America was a masterpiece. Six weeks before, a group totally unknown in America, they now had the number one single. With the help of Capitol, Epstein orchestrated it so that Beatlemania was on the ground (at JFK airport) the minute the band arrived. Who knows where the thousands of screaming fans came from but they were there and the arrival was reported on national television and in the press, further feeding the frenzy.

Over the years lots of artists had appeared on *The Ed Sullivan Show.* Fewer artists had appeared as top of the bill, but *no* artist had topped the bill for three consecutive Sunday nights. The first appearance was on Feb 9th 1964, and America was ready for their infectious pleasing sound. Three months previous to The Beatles' American debut, JFK, their young president, had been assassinated. America needed something to bring the smile back to their collective faces and they found that something in the form of The Beatles. The viewing figures for the first *Ed Sullivan Show* were the highest ever (73,000,000 viewers) and the crime figures were the lowest ever. That's where The Beatles' genius took over from Epstein's. It didn't matter how he did it. All he had to do was expose people to the music and the music would do the rest. The first song they performed on American Television was *All My Loving* and right there, in that magnificent two minutes and six seconds, their success was secured. But the best was yet to come!

They returned to a hero's welcome in the UK; BBC even interrupted their traditional Saturday sports programme, Grandstand, to include an airport interview with the conquering heroes.

5: They're Going To Put Me In The Movies:
A Hard Day's Night, Beatles For Sale and *Help!*

It's hard to realise now just how big The Beatles were. It was probably even harder in March 1964 to realise how big The Beatles were. Without the use of spin-doctors and a music industry intent on hyping pap idols they were (artistically and commercially) conquering the world. In March of 1964 the top five singles in America were:

1. Twist and Shout	The Beatles
2. Can't Buy Me Love	The Beatles
3. She Loves You	The Beatles
4. I Want To Hold Your Hand	The Beatles
5. Please Please Me	The Beatles.

Phenomenal!

The top five singles and four of them were Lennon & McCartney compositions.

On top of that, at the same time, The Beatles had additional singles at numbers 16,44,49,69,78,84 and 88!

That's twelve entries in the most important and lucrative music sales chart in the world. On top of which, *Meet The Beatles* had just become the biggest selling album in American history, having reached the 3,500,000 copies figure with no signs of slowing down.

Back home, in the UK, they hadn't been forgotten either. *Please Please Me* spent 33 weeks at the top of the UK album chart. *With The Beatles* knocked it from the top spot and that topped the chart for the next 21 weeks (*Please Please Me* sat in the number 2 spot for the first 20 weeks of this run). By that point The Beatles had held the number one spot in the UK album charts for a staggering 54 weeks. Then there was an eleven-week break, when an album by a London group featuring Lennon & McCartney's *I Wanna Be Your Man* topped the charts, and then it was back to The Beatles for their soundtrack album, *A Hard Day's Night,* which remained at the summit for the following 21 weeks.

Meanwhile, on the other side of the world, they'd created another first with the top six Australian singles, all Beatles singles. Back in London their effigies were moved into Madame Tussauds in London. Then they were off, with Jimmy Nicol standing in for an ill Ringo, to tour Japan.

During this running around, touring, making a movie and recording records, the Lennon & McCartney hit factory also managed, in the first six months of 1964, to write songs for other artists: *I'm In Love* and *Hello Little Girl* for the Fourmost; *A World Without Love,* a number one hit for Peter & Gordon and then their follow up, *Nobody I Know*; *Bad To Me*, *From A Window*, *I Call Your Name*, and *I'll Keep You Satisfied* for Billy J Kramer and the Dakotas. And of course there was the aforementioned *I Wanna Be Your Man* for the Rolling Stones; *Like Dreamers Do* for the Applejacks; *Love of The Loved* and *It's For You* especially for Cilla Black; *One And One Is Two* for The Strangers (with Mike Shannon); and finally Jazz diva, Ella Fitzgerald, who recorded *Can't Buy Me Love* and was rewarded with a UK hit.

When they returned from America, The Beatles reported immediately to Abbey Road Studios to record songs that would in part be the soundtrack to their first movie. Brian Epstein had secured a three-picture deal with United Artists. Again, it has been claimed that the manager didn't exactly tie up a great deal for The Beatles with United Artists, but again the important point to remember here is that he secured a deal for a movie we're still talking about forty years later!

Dick Lester, who had worked with the Goons and Spike Milligan, was hired to direct and Alun Owen was brought on board to write the script. Alun hung out with The Beatles for a few days, enjoying their mad and chaotic life and just observed every single thing that was happening to the Fabs. He then went away and came up with a script that was utter magic, in that it captured the essence of The Beatles' spirit and their individual personalities perfectly. Shot in black and white it still stands as the benchmark for other music artist-led feature films and has been pillaged repeatedly for ideas for video clips.

In the movie, The Beatles play themselves and are joined by Paul McCartney's screen grandfather (played by Wilfred 'Steptoe & Son' Brambell), who seems to spend his life scheming and trying to have everyone at each other's throats while seeking financial benefits from such conflicts. The Beatles two hapless (screen) tour managers try to keep the band together and out of trouble so that they can appear on a very important television show. Miraculously, and in spite of the grandfather, they make the final recording of the show by seconds and all's well that ends well.

In *A Hard Day's Night*, the film, The Beatles were compared to The Marx Brothers – probably because there were four of them and they were naturally very funny. It *is* The Beatles' finest movie. I remember the first time I went to see it, I experienced for the first time a cinema audience reacting vocally and energetically to everything that was happening up on the big screen.

Any time The Beatles were not needed on camera they would nip back to Abbey Road to continue work on the soundtrack. During these and earlier sessions they had recorded *Can't Buy Me Love*, which was written by John and Paul while they were on their recent visit to Miami, Florida, and *You Can't Do That. Can't Buy Me Love* is another excellent catchy Beatles classic. It had a presale of over a million in the UK and just over two million in America – another sales record. It was the first single to go straight to number one in both the UK and USA and topped the charts in most countries, becoming another major multi-million worldwide seller with over 70 covers by people ranging from Ella Fitzgerald to The Supremes.

The week that began on Monday 6th July 1964 was a big week. On the Monday, Beatles fans trying to catch a glimpse of their heroes as they arrived for the premiere of the movie, closed the West End of London. The movie was a major success both with the critics and at the box office. The movie had cost £200,000 and pretty soon it had grossed over £6,000,000 at the box office. On Friday 10th July 1964 both the single (Parlophone R5160) and album (Parlophone PMC 1230) *A Hard Day's Night* were released.

This is the only Beatles album that consists solely of Lennon & McCartney songs. On the early albums, they included the classic American covers from their live set and on the later albums George Harrison contributed a Northern Song or two. Lennon & McCartney's tunes had noticeably moved up another gear.

They probably knew that they had a huge and ever-expanding audience (sales of *Can't Buy Me Love* soon passed the 10,000,000 mark) awaiting their work and, unlike some who would have buckled under the pressure, they used it as a watershed. That's one of the incredible things about The Beatles: instead of destroying the band, their early success drove them on to greater artistic heights. At the time of *Can't Buy Me Love* many people, including myself, thought that they'd peaked, they'd never be able to better it. Then came the movie and thirteen new songs on the accompanying album, *A Hard Day's Night*.

The big thing about the songs was not so much that you grew to be familiar with them, but more that *they* were familiar with *you,* right from the first time you heard them. They all sounded like old friends immediately. A perfect example of this would be *I Should Have Known Better*. It was perfect pop, beautifully recorded with John Lennon vocally at his best, and it sounds as brilliant today as it did the day it was recorded. Before you have time to get over the magic of it, they hit you with *If I Fell*. Paul McCartney joined Lennon one verse with a soulful harmony and before the conclusion we had George adding the missing element to their then trademark harmony. The important blend of Beatles' voices worked so well because you had the character of George's heavy Scouse, warm singing voice, mixed with John and Paul's more American influenced voices – but it was the blend of all three that worked so well. Also it's worth noting here how well the acoustic guitars were recorded for this album. After *If I Fell* it was George's turn to step up to the mike to take lead vocals on *I'm Happy To Dance With You*. Another feel-good song, short and snappy, which shows that Lennon & McCartney didn't keep their best songs for themselves to sing. George took these gifts and made them his own. He confidently led the Fabs on this track and then stepped back from the spotlight to let Paul take over lead vocals on *And I Love Her*. But although Paul sang the song it was George's masterly guitar work and solo that made the recording the gem it is.

Those last four songs - starting with *I Should Have Know Better*, *If I Fell*, *I'm Happy Just To Dance With You* and ending with *And I Love Her* - constitute the best four-track sequence I've ever heard. I don't mean that the tracks on either side of them are slouches either; with this four track selection they'd created perfect pop music, and nothing could have been bettered. This is a classic pop album, thirteen superb songs – all from the Lennon & McCartney song writing partnership.

Following this, they could have rested on their laurels and just repeated this formula for the remainder of their career. But there was something driving The Beatles. It could have been the natural bond between John and Paul, because both of them had lost their mothers early in life; it could have been the fact that their friend and early band member Stuart Sutcliffe died; it could even have been in some way due to the fact that as Northerners they were initially resisted and given such a hard time by the Southern-led music business; it could have had something to do with the fact that they were such huge music fans themselves and knew all their favourite music inside out; it could have something to do with the fact that the four of them probably realised they could either make a mark as a Beatle or, as a part-time musician, spend the remainder of their lives with nothing more than the dole to look forward to; or it could have been, encouraged by Epstein and Martin, that they were aware of the potential greatness that was theirs for the taking; it could even have had to do with the fact that Epstein had failed in the army, failed at RADA, hadn't exactly been inspired or taxed running his father's store, and so more than anything he didn't want to suffer yet another failure, this time with The Beatles.

It could have been any of those things or, indeed, it could have been a combination of all, or maybe they were just blindly making the music they loved and all of the rest was a by-product. But whatever it was, you got the feeling that once they'd achieved any level of success, they'd immediately set their sights higher and, in order to satisfy their own needs, they'd keep on going towards pastures new.

Even the soundtrack songs that weren't used in the movie were superlative, and songs like the snappy *Any Time At All*, the ode to lost love *I'll Cry Instead*, the pensive *Things We Said Today* or *You Can't Do That,* with John Lennon singing his heart out, had all past the test of time with flying colours.

They dashed off to the States for the biggest tour (then) ever undertaken by an international artist, playing to between 14,000 and 32,000 people per night, and then returned in time for the release of their new single, *I Feel Fine* (Parlophone R5200, released on Friday 27th November 1964). *I Feel Fine* showed John Lennon inventing and using guitar feedback for the first time, an accident he probably happened upon while recording, but one which was going to give Jimi Hendrix a career. The B-side was *She's A Woman,* with McCartney showing he could be as raunchy as Lennon as he belted out this catchy rocker. The single was another smash hit, selling a million in both the UK and the USA almost immediately.

In keeping with George Martin and Brian Epstein's plan for two albums a year and EMI's desperate need for an album for the all-important Christmas market, The Beatles returned to the Abbey Road studios less than two months after they'd concluded work on *A Hard Day's Night* to start work on their fourth album, *Beatles For Sale.*

Beatles For Sale (Parlophone PMC 1240, released on 4th December 1964) also went straight to number one. I still find it an uncomfortable album to listen to. Of course there has to be one album you like less than the others, hasn't there? To me it sounds like an album that was put together in a hurry for the Christmas market. Even the title appeared like a throwaway or a clue. Which is all very unfair because there are some classics on it. All the Lennon & McCartney songs for instance; they're all beautifully simple, well-crafted songs. One song, *No Reply,* for example, was reported at one time a contender for a single and rightly so. The sad and emotional *I'm A Loser* could also have been a single and then the irresistible *Eight Days a Week;* the soulful *Baby's In Black;* the big ballad, *I'll Follow The Sun;* the cheeky *Every Little Thing;* the self-effacing *I Don't Want to Spoil The Party;* and the innovative-sounding *What You're Doing* all worked incredibly well and still do, it's just that by this time they'd just outgrown the *covers* and you have to think (with what we knew came later) that this could have been another classic album if they'd not had to rush it into the shops, if they'd taken their time and finished it instead with another half a dozen Lennon & McCartney classics. Wishful thinking, but then again as my mother always used to say, wish in one hand and pee in the other and see which one fills first. It was a stopgap album from a band that was clearly above stopgaps. Having said that, it was definitely worth the price, if only to hear John Lennon's amazing vocals on *Mr Moonlight,* with Paul McCartney wringing every last ounce of drama from the performance with his work on the Hammond Organ.

The Beatles continued to work their way through the covers from their live set with Buddy Holly, Chuck Berry, Lieber & Stroller and Carl Perkins (two songs) all receiving writing credits on this album, which enjoyed a definite country music flavour. The album went straight to number one, replacing *A Hard Day's Night*. Just to show how much the chart had changed since they'd first entered it four albums and just a mere eighteen months before, here's that week's top ten.

1. Beatles For Sale	The Beatles
2. A Hard Day's Night	The Beatles
3. The Rolling Stones	The Rolling Stones
4. 12 Songs of Christmas	Jim Reeves
5. The Kinks	The Kinks
6. Pretty Woman	Roy Orbison
7. Moonlight and Roses	Jim Reeves
8. The Animals	The Animals
9. Five Faces Of	Manfred Man
10. Aladdin and his Lamp	Cliff Richard & The Shadows

The Beatles had totally changed the flavour and style of the charts in about a year and a half. They had released four mega selling albums, which had topped the charts all around the world, and they'd never once taken their foot off the pedal.

It's interesting how artists, including some pretenders to the throne, work nowadays. They'll clear the decks; spend up to a year writing or finding the material and then from six months to a year recording. Then they'll release it six months later and then tour and promote it for a couple of months before taking time off for nervous and physical exhaustion before starting the cycle all over again. The Beatles wrote and recorded material for seven singles, four albums, made a movie, appeared on numerous televisions, radio shows and concert stages all over the world in a whirlwind eighteen months, but that's not important; what's important is the consistency and lasting quality of their work while inside this hurricane.

And it wasn't to stop there. Something else happened at this point, or should I say that *someone* else happened at this point, and his name was Bob Dylan. His UK career launch was helped no end by the praise he received from The Beatles – particularly John Lennon and George Harrison. Both Dylan and The Beatles were demonstrating that your songs could be used to put your point of view across; that's as well as for the listeners' enjoyment of course. The Beatles and Bob Dylan were to give songs and writing credibility never before experienced.

Over Christmas 1964, The Beatles did their hugely successful, third and final London Christmas show, this time at The Hammersmith Odeon and titled, 'Another Beatles Christmas Show'.

Then came 1965 and it was time for their second movie and a soundtrack album to accompany it. Unlike their first experience, this wasn't quite so pleasant and, although they considered making a Western movie and a *Lord Of the Rings* project, this was to be their last feature. The problem was the script. Whereas Alun Owen had watched The Beatles to discover that the secret in transferring the magic on to the big screen was to allow them to be themselves, in their second movie, *Help!,* they were required to act. Big Mistake.

Ringo is sent a ring by a fan from the other side of the world. The ring turns out to be a sacrificial ring, essential for a ritual. A gang of thugs are sent out to recover the ring, eventually having to kidnap Ringo. He and the other three escape and they try to remove the ring at a laboratory during their visit to the Alps. Unsuccessful, they return to England, with the gang still in pursuit, and seek the help of New Scotland Yard. Next they head to the Bahamas where Ringo discovers the formula to remove the ring and everyone lives happily every after. The script was a disaster. Maybe it was meant to be the first draft for the BBC Television's *Holiday Show*. Whatever it was, it should not have been used as the basis for their second movie. But then, perhaps again it served as a movie lesson that Elvis Presley had sadly never learned.

On the other hand, their next single was a complete revelation. It was *Ticket To Ride* coupled with *Yes It Is* (Parlophone R5265, released on Friday 9th April 1965). The B-side was another classic ballad in the style of *This Boy* and again could have been a single in its own right. *Ticket To Ride* sees the bang getting adventurous in the studio. Up until now, most of their recording were based on live versions of their songs; versions that they could have reproduced note by note for stage, but now, encouraged by their phenomenal success, they were interested in how far they could push themselves and the recording procedure. Paul added lead guitar breaks at the end of the middle eight sections which gave The Beatles another first; twin lead guitars. *Ticket To Ride* topped the charts in every country that released records!

The Beatles had rejected the first suggestion for the movie title, *Eight Arms To Hold You*, in favour of *Help!* They were asked to write a song in this name. They did; it was a song where John very definitely sang lead vocals. It was a marked departure from what to do when a boy loses a girl or boy loves girl/loses girl/wins girl that had been the norm. It was altogether more of a cry for help, much more confessional and autobiographical than before.

Outside influences were starting to have an effect, which were forcing The Beatles – particularly the songwriters – to become introspective. This was a time when the sad death of President Kennedy was a recent memory and The Beatles had a few scares from crazies themselves while touring America. People felt that The Beatles had special powers, which could heal the crippled and cure the sick; people were always trying to get close too close to them. When they turned up at gigs there'd be droves of people in wheelchairs waiting for them. On top of which, a band that had once prided themselves on their live shows were no longer able to hear themselves on stage above the fans screaming. George Martin likened the noise to that of Boeing 747 Jumbo Jet taking off.

Help! the single (Parlophone R6305) was released on Friday 23rd July 1965 with the amazing toe tapping dance floor filler *I'm Down* on the B-side. Again, number one everywhere bar the moon. The movie opened up that same week to mixed reviews but a great box office. No matter how weak the script, people were still impressed with the naturalness of the Fabs.

Help! the album (Parlophone PC1255, released on Friday 6th August 1965) is not a classic album but neither is it another stopgap like *Beatles For Sale.* It was an album they needed to make to get from *A Hard Day's Night* to *Rubber Soul.* If *Help!* was a John-sung classic then Paul hadn't been hanging around feeling sorry for himself. With *Yesterday,* a solo effort (Paul on vocals and acoustic guitar and accompanied by a string quartet), he introduced a song which was to become the most covered Beatles song and quite possibly the most covered song of popular music of all times, with over 2500 versions in existence. It was released in America under McCartney's name and sold over a million copies; it won the Ivor Novello Award for the most outstanding song of the year. People like Otis Redding, Nat King Cole, Perry Como, Cilla Black, Pat Boone, Marianne Faithfull, Tom Jones, Smokey Robinson and The Miracles and Frank Sinatra all covered it.

The last two songs to be covered by The Beatles appeared on *Help!* First there was *Act Naturally* and then the Larry Williams showstopper, *Dizzy Miss Lizzy.*

George Harrison had two songs on *Help!* The first one *I Need You,* which featured the wah-wah pedal (volume control foot pedal) for the first time. The second was the very melodic and singalong-able *You Like Me Too Much* with John, Paul and George Martin all on piano.

The Lennon & McCartney songs are all beautiful vintage songs, which you felt sure were your friends the first time you heard them. I just love the blend of voices on the gorgeous *I've Just Seen A Face.* You get the feeling of an extra voice created by the blend of John, Paul and George's voices singing together. This unique sound, I believe, was part of the reason for their success. Groups like the Beach Boys and the Hollies had close harmonies, but both these groups lacked the soul of The Beatles. The lift The Beatles give their record when those combined voices come in is quite incredible, quite spiritual.

Another Girl, You're Going To Lose That Girl, The Night Before, It's Only Love, and *Tell Me What You See* all show the band growing in stature as performers and, particularly, as recording artists with Lennon & McCartney as writers on safe lyrical ground. But with *You've Got To Hide Your Love Away* John Lennon had Dylan sitting on his shoulder, as he is as honest as it was possible to be as a married man in the sixties. This song was also a hit for Silkie, another of Epstein's groups, and John and Paul produced the session with Paul also adding acoustic guitar to it. The Fabs broke one of their golden rules by including singles – both *Ticket To Ride* and *Help!* – on the album. The album topped the charts for three months. The Beatles' reign was continuing unchallenged.

6: The Studio Years: *Rubber Soul & Revolver*

On Sunday 15th August 1965 The Beatles broke the world record for attendance and box office gross when they played to 55,600 fans at the Shea Stadium. It's interesting now to look at the Shea Stadium video; the look of love and adulation in every member of the audience's eyes is nothing short of incredible. I suppose, in a small way, it goes to show exactly what The Beatles meant to their fans. I think it's fair to say that a lot of the fans were living their lives for The Beatles. Just over $300,000 was taken at the box office and The Beatles received a reported $160,000 (then £57,000) fee. To put that salary into perspective, I should tell you that rarely do artists achieve anywhere near that sort of fee all these years later at the beginning of the new millennium. As well as adding seriously to their coffers, the Shea Stadium show also just happened to be yet another nail in the touring coffin. As already mentioned, their audiences were so loud that The Beatles were unable to hear themselves perform, so they were fast losing their edge as a live band.

Added to which, they were starting to have more of a say in their career decisions.

And if that wasn't enough, when The Beatles started out their contemporaries were artists like Freddie and the Dreamers, Gerry and The Pacemakers, The Fourmost, The Applejacks, The Dakotas, The Tremeloes and the Dave Clark Five, but by August of 1965, when they returned from America and started to consider their sixth album, the charts were alive with more contemporary artists like The Animals, the Kinks, Them, The Small Faces and The Who on the UK front, and from America people like The Byrds (who admitted basing their sound on The Beatles' twelve string guitar sound); Dylan had crashed the UK chart barrier and even the Beach Boys, after a shaky start, were starting to show their potential; a potential Paul McCartney would always keep a close eye on.

On their return from America, they took a six-week break, their longest break since John, Paul and George first started working together in February 1958. They regrouped in Abbey Road Studios on Tuesday 12th October 1965 to start work on their new album, which was due in the stores for that year's ever-important Christmas market; then as now December accounted for the majority of the year's record sales. Free from the once heavy touring schedule they spent their longest amount of time to date recording an album – October 12th 1965 to November 15th 1965. Free from feeling the necessity to perform these songs live, they started to build up and experiment with enhancing the songs through production and arrangements.

The Beatles were by now a multi-million pound business, single-handedly doing wonders for Britain's overseas trade figures, a fact acknowledged by Prime Minster Harold Wilson, when they were individually awarded the MBE by the Queen on 26th October 1965. Sadly Wilson and his government's generosity was not extended to Brian Epstein, although The Beatles quipped that they thought MBE stood for **Mr Brian Epstein**.

Less than six weeks later they released both single and album to an eager worldwide audience. What a treat was in store for the unsuspecting public. *We Can Work It Out* & *Day Tripper* (Parlophone R 5389, released on Friday 3rd December 1965) was a double A-sided single, which shot straight to number one everywhere, as did the new album *Rubber Soul* (Parlophone PMC 1627) which was released on the same day.

Day Tripper was supposedly about drug taking in general and Paul McCartney's alleged reluctance in particular, but it still worked more universally as a song about a girl who was a tease. It's a very catchy song, composed around a bass-riff. This was a record only The Beatles could have made. They were starting to create a unique sound but a unique sound that was not restricted by the constraints of musical styles. Paul sang the flip side, *We Can Work It Out*, which was the side that got the attention, and the number one chart position, in the US of A. A plea in vain to a disappearing girlfriend but a plea that worked with the fans on this million selling single. Otis Redding showed the full worth and variety of the song when his punchy brass driven version reached the top ten in the UK (March 1967). Stevie Wonder did a magic version of *We Can Work It Out* in the early seventies which was also a big hit in the US and UK.

We Can Work it Out together with *Day Tripper* was the first single to have a promotional video clip. Again, necessity proved to be the mother of invention. The Beatles didn't have time to travel all around the world appearing on television to promote their new singles, so the Fab Four came up with a novel idea. They decided to make their own little mini television show, featuring, in this instance, visual performances of both titles on their new double A-sided single and then send the clips to television stations around the world. Like all great ideas, it was so simple you'd have to wonder why someone hadn't already thought of it. The clip was used on numerous television shows from *Top of The Pops* in the UK to *The Ed Sullivan Show* in the US, where the talismanic Ringo had recorded a special message to go with the songs. At the same time as filming the above clips in Twickenham, they also recorded clips for *Help!*, *Ticket To Ride*, and *I Feel Fine* for distribution.

Rubber Soul is still, to me, a flawless gem. The Beatles, in their development were giving much-needed value for money to the fans and credibility to the art of making albums. Frustrated at no longer being able to show the world how great they were on stage, they wanted to make amends with their recorded work. As I mentioned before, The Beatles were already singlehandedly responsible for changing the album format from a record company cash-in to a valid art form. With *Rubber Soul* they pushed the boundaries even further.

Purely and simply, *Rubber Soul* is a beautiful album; I still enjoy it as much today as I did the day it was released. It's certainly one of my favourite Beatles albums and in a way, it's quite remarkable that the album should enjoy all of these qualities, especially when you consider that it was both written and recorded under severe time pressure. *Rubber Soul* sees The Beatles take another major confident step into their brave new world.

Just look at their photo on the album sleeve, taken by Robert Freeman. They look healthier, stronger and fresher, and gone are the boyish features of earlier sleeves and photos. John, ever the one to challenge, is the only member of the group looking the camera (the audience) in the eye. The Beatles are not mentioned on the front of the sleeve. I mean that's really incredible; they were now so BIG that they didn't need to put their name on the album sleeve! The sleeve photo is elongated because as the photographer was showing the band slides of the photograph, the white card he was using as a backdrop to project onto slid backwards. The band were so excited by the distorted image that they shouted, 'That's it, that's the sleeve. We'd like it to look exactly like that.' It's also interesting to note from the numerous casual photographs on the back of the sleeve, that the old mop top and their smart collarless suits had been replaced by a more casual, comfortable and individual dress sense.

The title came from Paul McCartney and was coined to describe white Anglo-Saxons playing American Soul music. *Rubber Soul* the album and the fourteen songs contained therein were simply and honestly the results of four chaps from Liverpool – with their innovative producer – hitting their stride and leaving the pack far behind.

The album starts off with *Drive My Car*; The Beatles having fun and happy not to take themselves too seriously, particularly with the humorous phrase sung by the backing vocalists, George, Paul & John; 'Beep Beep' and 'Beep Beep Yeah.' The second song is the ground breaking *Norwegian Wood (This Bird Has Flown)* in which John (lyrically) deals with an (alleged) romance with an actress who was (apparently) giving him (a) a hard time by not letting him have it all his own way and (b) a great idea for a song. John dressed the situation up cleverly so that the still-unforgiving society of the sixties, and more particularly his wife, wouldn't be cute to the real facts. *Norwegian Wood* is a song inspired and influenced by Dylan's work. It's easy to nitpick at John's lyrics now, but you have to remember in the sixties divorce was still a taboo subject and not the dating tactic it's now become. Divorcees carried a cloak of shame and unlike most people who would only have to deal with three families at most, in John Lennon's case we're talking about a man who was one of the favourite sons of the entire English Nation.

To this lyrical twist, you add a heart-tugging folk-style melody and George Harrison demonstrating his newfound love of Indian Music on an instrument called a sitar, which was making its debut in recorded western music.

George, like the other Beatles, was very adventurous in that he was into everything musical. He grew up liking Elvis Presley, Chuck Berry and George Formby. *Meatballs* was the first song he could remember paying attention to. He was particularly impressed and influenced by Buddy Holly's choice of unorthodox chord progressions in his music. The innovative guitarist spent a lot of times painstakingly working out the guitar part on *Be Bop A Lou*. From then on, he would dissect the guitar parts on the records he listened to. This diligence and attention to detail served him well when it came to working out his own guitar parts. George was unusual as a lead guitarist in that he didn't have a set formula or band sound he'd try to fit everything he played into. He would come up with some incredibly unusual guitar parts, which were like solutions to puzzles and separate singalong songs within the songs. They were very memorable, melodic, catchy, pleasing and even at times cheeky. While working on the *A Hard Day's Night* film, George met and married Patti Boyd, who turned him on to Indian mysticism. Out of that culture, he discovered an album called *Portrait of a Genius* by Ravi Shankar and from there he discovered the sitar which he immediately started to study under the wing of the same Ravi Shankar. Although George Harrison would probably have disagreed, a few months later he was playing this complex instrument competently on a Beatles' song.

Can you imagine what it must have been like in the Abbey Road Studios during October and November 1965, not to mention the next few years? You had The Beatles and all of their influences, new and old; George Martin with his vast wealth of classical music and his experience of making music; the technical back-up team of engineers and tape ops (operators) who were continually being pushed to their limits with all the experimentation as the five principals developed and requested, 'Could you find a way of making this sound like a roundabout at a funfair.' It was very much a creative melting pot, and a melting pot which inspired true greatness from all those involved. Meanwhile the rest of us just looked (and listened) in awe.

The Word doesn't really work as well as the same sentiment worked on the later *All You Need Is Love*. It's just a wee bit too awkward or stiff, maybe even a wee bit ahead of its time. On the other hand the magnificently arranged and performed *Nowhere Man* works perfectly – another lost single? *Michelle* is the Paul song on a predominately John album. It's very much in the vein of *Yesterday,* with the band singing part of the lyrics in French. This is the most covered song from *Rubber Soul* with both Overlanders and David and Jonathan simultaneously enjoying UK chart success. The Overlanders' version reached number one and gave them their one and only UK hit record. David and Jonathan's version on the other hand peaked at number 11, but their consolation was that they were to have another bigger hit, *Lovers Of The World Unite*, a few months later.

George showed his song writing was developing perfectly. It must have been difficult for George in those days. You are in the same band as the best writing team that, quite possibly, the world has ever known. And you've got to bring your songs to the same table. Add to that the pressure that you don't have a John or a Paul (like they had each other) to help you finish a difficult bit, or even co-write it with. The fact that the man managed to get songs on Beatles albums at all is a major achievement in itself and George still had a few classic surprises hidden up his sleeve. George's two tunes on *Rubber Soul* were *Think For Yourself*, with Paul playing a fuzz bass, and *If I Needed Someone*.

The Hollies covered and had a hit with *If I Needed Someone*. The Hollies also worked on close harmony arrangements and, technically, they probably were perfect but, perhaps because they were trying so hard to get it perfect, the majority of their singles sounded like vocal exercises, whereas The Beatles' blend appeared to be so effortless, yet still powerfully soulful and rarely more soulful than on *In My Life*. This is one of my all time favourite songs, written mostly by John, with Paul adding the middle eight after John had completed the rest of it in his house. At that time, they rarely sat down and wrote a song together, although both would still make valuable contribution to each other's material. George Harrison claimed this was one of his favourite Beatles songs and you can tell by his economic melodic contributions that he was obviously inspired by the whole sentiment. Lyrically speaking, this song started out as a trip though Liverpool, reflecting on all the childhood places like Penny Lane and Strawberry Fields. For whatever reason, the lyric didn't sit comfortably with John who chose instead to bare his soul, leaving the vivid Liverpool scenes to the future with a song like *Strawberry Fields Forever*.

In My Life shows how important Martin had become in The Beatles' creative process. His superb baroque piano break is the final piece in the beautiful arrangement that elevates the record into the rarefied land of classics. Martin's piano was recorded with the tape running at half speed and then replayed at full speed, giving a kind of harpsichord effect. It's a very moving song and one that never fails to tug at the heartstrings. I think it's because we can all put ourselves in the position of the song's orator, trying to accept life's disappointments and lost loves. Again, as with all the great songs, it's short and it's simple with no space wasted on repeating lines. George on guitar and John and Paul on vocals bring it to a very moving climax.

Listening to *Rubber Soul*, as in fact I do while writing this, it sounds like a masterly piece of work, with all the songs working together perfectly, each one in its right place. This, the running order of the songs, was still a George Martin chore although by now The Beatles were taking more of an interest in the post-recording process of mixing and sequencing the songs. Mixing down the songs in order to achieve the perfect balance between instruments and voices is a very skilful process. For example, should a guitar, piano, drums or voice be out of balance with their counterparts, the net result can ruin the whole flow of the song. The song only works as a record if nothing is allowed to distract you from its natural rhythm and flow. Equally, if the songs are not placed in a correct sequence, the album can drag, lose its pace and become unsatisfying. This vital work is what George Martin and his Abbey Road team were masters at, as is evident by how much we still love and enjoy The Beatles' albums.

It should not be forgotten here that we, the fans, sometimes grow out of our once favourite music. For whatever reason, it just doesn't move with you anymore and, through the passing of time, it becomes dated and the sounds become annoying rather than offering the pleasure they once did. In the case of The Beatles, at least for me, this is never the case. I love all their albums (all the ones I consider to be true Beatles' albums, but I'll get into that later), without exception. The recorded works pass the acid test of time and are all timeless treasures. This is quite incredible, especially when you consider how antiquated the recording equipment and procedures were in the early days. It must be put down equally to the quality and the performance of the songs and the manner in which they were committed to tape.

Rubber Soul appears as though all the songs were written around the same time to come together to make this album. But such was the pressure of getting the record ready for that all important Christmas ship-date that, as they neared their deadline, The Beatles, and their producer, realised they only had thirteen songs instead of their traditional, value for money, fourteen. So, they retrieved from the vaults at Abbey Road a song they'd recorded for *Help!* but for whatever reason hadn't included on that album. The song was *Wait* and they did a bit more work on the vocals. Then, as if by magic, they had their album completed *literally* within minutes of their deadline.

The album, their sixth, went straight to number one in the charts only ten days after they finished recording. I bet that would have brought smiles to all the EMI bods now that their Christmas bonuses were assured, thanks once again to George Martin's Liverpudlian discovery. You'd think they would have looked after Gentleman George Martin properly, wouldn't you? No way. Profits are profits and although The Beatles were filling the EMI coffers by millions upon millions, their producer was still a salaried member of EMI staff and shared none of these profits. Somewhat disgruntled, George Martin left to set up his own company and studio, AIR, and continued to work with The Beatles as an independent producer.

Brian Epstein for his part chose this time to renegotiate The Beatles' record royalty rate. EMI, hoping to keep their most successful breadwinners happy, hiked the royalty up by a staggering 650%. What this did of course was to make The Beatles less dependent on the phenomenal income the continuous touring generated. Sadly for Brian, this, in turn, lessened his role in the most successful entertainment act the world had ever known.

Rubber Soul was as I say, a peak, but not a peak they were prepared to sit back and bask in the glory of. They played a very short UK tour over

Christmas 1965 when their UK fee reached £1,000 a night for the first time. Then it was time to get back to the records.

Paperback Writer was by Paul McCartney, with a little help from his friend John Lennon. The song was meant to be about John Lennon, the author. John's second book, *A Spaniard In The Works*, was to be published on June 24th 1966, two weeks to the day after the release of this new single. *Paperback Writer* was another story song with references to a few characters including one whose name sounded not unlike how Paul's name would have sounded were it to be recorded backwards. Paul was trying to show that The Beatles could compete with his current favourite group, the Beach Boys, on vocal harmonies. He didn't have to try to show he was a great bass player; it is more than evident with his playing the classic bass-riff this song is based upon. The flip side was *Rain,* which showed the hints of psychedelia creeping in, especially with the first use of vocals recorded backwards (perhaps how the above mentioned character name originated) and yet another number one single.

As I mentioned earlier, *Rubber Soul* was to be the first step in substituting a new medium to fill the impending gap due to be left in their lives by the lack of touring. Despite this newfound space, they were still under pressure of time, release deadlines, television and occasional concerts as they completed work on *Rubber Soul.* Not so with *Revolver.* This album was recorded between 8th April 1966 and 22nd June 1966. This was towards the end of a gap that would prove to be their longest break from gigging since the days of the Quarrymen.

Originally in this period The Beatles were meant to be working on their third movie, a western, which was to be based on the novel *A Kind of Loving,* by Richard Condon. The movie was to have had a country and western feel and the boys were meant to come up with some country songs to reflect this. The Beatles (particularly Ringo, who was looking forward to playing a Mexican) liked the book and gave their nod to the project but they were very disappointed with the first script presented. The project moved on to the back burner, eventually it was dropped all together. This, in turn, allowed the decks to be completely cleared and so, with trusted and creative producer, Gentleman George Martin, they started work on the new recordings, which were to produce the *Paperback Writer & Rain* single and *Revolver* album.

If *Rubber Soul* was a John song-led album, then *Revolver* is a Paul song-led album and a damned fine album at that. To be honest, it took me a while to get to grips with the music on *Revolver.* Now, when I look back on it, I keep thinking it had something to do with the sleeve; Revolver is my least favourite Beatles' sleeve. I have to admit that I'm not a fan of black and white photos, artwork, or movies at the best of times. Add to that, the fact that Klaus Voormann's artwork (literally) leaves me a bit cold. This left me with a sleeve I had to get beyond before I could enjoy the music within, initially my loss. They say perseverance pays; well it did with this album. It's now up there in my top three Beatles' albums.

The album starts off with a George Harrison song, *Taxman*. At this point in their career, The Beatles where paying tax at a staggering rate of 19 shillings and 6 pence (97 & 1/2 new pence) in the pound. Newly wed George, tongue firmly in cheek, for it was he who signed (on behalf of The Beatles) the cheques to the Inland Revenue, is having a bit of a go at our taskmasters. He's very amusing and articulate in his criticism. *Taxman* is one of the first protest pop songs, even before Dylan and Lennon, and benefits from a blindingly innovative and short guitar solo from Paul McCartney.

George and his new bride, Patti Boyd, took a holiday in Spain with Brian Epstein. Brian obviously gave his client a bit of a pep talk about the old song writing, because George has an unprecedented three songs on the *Revolver* album, and, spurred on by the confidence of this, he was writing and stockpiling a lot of the songs which would make up his first solo effort, *All Things Must Pass*. His other two *Revolver* songs *Love To You* and *I Want To Tell You* sound perfect under The Beatles' umbrella, proving no preferential treatment was afforded to the Lennon & McCartney songs.

Paul had written another song, *Woman*, for his mates Peter and Gordon, and he had the song credited under the name Bernard Webb to see if the song could be a hit merely on the strength of the quality of the song rather than through The Beatles connection. He needn't have worried because it was a chart success both here and in the States. As a writer his future was secure even outside of The Beatles. His song writing for the band was still on the rise and a long way from peaking, although some of us wondered, would he ever be able to better *Eleanor Rigby*?

Eleanor Rigby benefited immensely from George Martin's exquisite string arrangement in which he used a double string quartet, or something similar. Lyrically it's among Paul's best work, taking us immediately into the middle of this mini-movie during which all these characters come to life through the words and the music. This is very important in trying to create a story in a song. You don't have the luxury of time and pages to fill out all the subtleties of the scene and the characters. The melody of a song and the mood created by the vocalist will however take you to a place that descriptive words rarely will. It could be argued that *Eleanor Rigby* is the work of a genius.

With this song you discover all about the life and soul of one Ms Rigby and how all may not be as it seems. You see this girl, perhaps beautiful, picking up the rice in a church where a wedding has been and you get to go behind the beauty and see some of the troubles. The more you listen to this song, the more you are encouraged to fill out a bit more of the movie that Paul started. It was obviously an idea that worked very successfully because at least two hundred artists covered it, including The Supremes, Four Tops, Johnny Mathis, Vanilla Fudge, whose dramatic sound worked well on the song, Ray Charles, who scored a UK Top 30 hit with it, and the soul Queen, Aretha Franklin, who enjoyed a US Top 30 with this truly beautiful song.

Revolver is The Beatles at their creative peak; three years and a million planets from *Please Please Me. Rubber Soul*, I suppose, showed us that they were capable of scaling incredible heights. With *Revolver* however, they created an album against which all future albums would be judged. In the middle of this creative whirlpool you had the four musicians; you had producer George Martin; you had engineer, Geoff Emerick; you had Lennon and McCartney, the world's finest songwriters; with George Harrison proving the finest didn't have a monopoly on northern songs; you had studio electronic experimentation; you had stimulants (chemical and otherwise); you had an explosion in the fashion and pop art worlds; you had the frustrations of touring and living continuously in a fish bowl (yes it was *gold*fish bowl, but it was not rewarding in the non-monetary sense) and, on top of all of that, you had a host of emerging artists: Dylan, The Beach Boys, The Kinks, The Spencer Davies Group, Jimi Hendrix's Experience, and Ulster's finest, Them, chomping at the bit. All were ready, willing, but unable to steal The Beatles' crown.

Some of them even tried to get there using songs from the *Revolver* album. Cliff Bennett and The Rebel Rousers enjoyed a hit with another Beatles song, *Got To Get You Into My Life;* it reached number six in the UK Top Ten during late August 1966 (around the same time The Beatles held the number one position with *Eleanor Rigby*) with Paul producing the cover version of his Tamla Motown-influenced classic. On The Beatles' version, the brass section is from Georgie Fame's band, The Blue Flames. This punchy song proved that The Beatles could do what the other English artists were failing miserably to do - reproduce the American soul sound. The Beatles' version was released some years later as a single in the US of A. It was at the time of the Charles Manson Murders when Manson was giving heavy publicity to *Helter Skelter*, by calling his 'mission' after The Beatles' song. Good old Capitol Records stuck *Helter Sketler* on the B-side of *Got To Get you Into My Life* to 'Capitolise' on the infamous Manson. It reached Number 3 in the American charts.

Paul McCartney has often said how much he loved the Beach Boys, particularly their song *God Only Knows*. This influence he proudly demonstrates with the beautiful *Here, There and Everywhere*. I love listening to this song; there is so little instrumentation on the record that all you really get is the song and that incredible blend of Beatles' voices. It was no surprise that someone with a voice as pure as Emmylou Harris would record this song and in so doing enjoy a UK Top 30 hit.

Everybody's younger brother or sister loved *Yellow Submarine*, which was another track on the *Revolver* album. This song, purely and simply, was written and recorded for the enjoyment of children. All children could sing this song from start to finish, even making a brave attempt at all the silly sounds in between as well. This was the first time we were to hear Ringo singing on a Beatles single (another Double A-side and another number one single). The vocal chorus is provided by Mal Evans, Neil Aspinall, Brian Jones, Marianne Faithful, Patti Harrison, George Martin with John Lennon keeping them all in time (and amused) by blowing bubbles with his latest musical discovery - glass, water and straw! The kids around the streets of Ulster had their own version of this song. It went, 'We all eat Stork Margarine, Stork Margarine, Stork...'

The influence of chemicals is rarely more apparent than on *She Said She Said*, a John song and definitely a drug-influenced song. Peter Fonda had dropped a tab of acid in Beatles' company and thought he had died. As he came down from the influence of the drug he ran around saying he knew what it felt like to be dead, a unique lyrical idea, which John immediately picked up on.

The songs on this album, one after another, were truly brilliant and totally diverse, yet for some reason they all worked perfectly together. I can't imagine anyone being brave enough now to put Yellow *Submarine* on a record that shares gems like *Here, There and Everywhere,* not to mention *And Your Bird Can Sing*. But I believe that was part of their secret. They weren't musical snobs. They were, first and foremost, songwriters in the classic tradition. Songs were meant to be for entertainment, to console you, to comfort you and to make you laugh. Songs were not written simply to make money. A by-product of successfully writing songs was that they generated income, but in The Beatles' case this proved to be simply because the songwriters were being successful at their art. They were communicating with people and people were responding. The public loved The Beatles' songs so they bought the records. It was that simple.

Just look at all the other stuff being put out, and look at all the other groups. Why, out of all the Liverpool groups, all the British groups, all the artists in the world even, why would The Beatles be the most successful and sell the most records and, even after all these years, still be selling the most records?

The answer is simple. They wrote and performed *great* songs.

Yes, they also made cracking records, they had a brilliant producer, a highly competent manager, a superb road crew, they looked cute, played as well as anyone else in the land, and were professional, very professional. But all of this would have been meaningless if they didn't have great songs for their foundation. They certainly still wouldn't be selling records today in the volumes they do, because of fashion, or coolness, or clever marketing. When was the last time you saw an advertisement for a Beatles record? But people, old and young, still react to the phenomenal body of work which they left and it will, I believe, serve as their testament for ever after - and a bit more.

Even today, perhaps more than any of the other albums, I'm finding *Revolver* to be maturing with age. Every time I put it on I know and savour the joy in store for me, but it's not a nostalgic thing. The record still excites me, still involves me, and still pulls me into the songs. As one song finishes, I can hear the opening bars of the next one, before it even starts.

The songs are like old friends; friends you still enjoy rather than tolerate because of your history. *Dr Robert* comes on and I immediately think of John Lennon and his search for Dr Robert, the New York City doctor who kept all his friends from being ill by keeping them high. Or *For No One*, a Paul song that was a personal favourite of both John and George (neither of whom actually played on the track). Its innovative French Horn solo was hummed by Paul to George Martin who, in turn, scored it so that Alan Civil could play it.

Even the song that *Revolver* closes with, *Tomorrow Never Knows*, leaves you hooked, intrigued and hungry for what they were to do next.

50

It's an experimental song, written by John with a little help from *The Tibetan Book of the Dead*, some chemical substances and a few influences from Dr Timothy Leary. The magic is that, no matter how alien all of the above might be to you, the song is structured and the record produced in such a way that it carries you along on John's journey of discovery. Funny how, in the middle of all these illustrious people, places and things that it would be the down-to-earth Ringo who would come up with the most cosmic song title on the album. He'd been meaning to say *Tomorrow Never Comes* but his tongue flipped the 'Comes' to 'Knows' and John had the title for his enlightening song journey.

It wasn't a song like Paul's *Eleanor Rigby*. Neither would it ever achieve anything like *Eleanor Rigby's* 200 cover versions, but the variety it offered to *Revolver,* along with, say, *Yellow Submarine*, is what entertained us, is what made The Beatles the complete band. And just in case we thought we had them sussed, they had another major box of tricks they were waiting to open for us.

Although not a deciding factor in how things turned out for The Beatles on the live stage, it surely was an ominous sign when 1966 started off with the closing of the Cavern Club in Liverpool with debts of £10,000. The Cavern had been their old stomping ground and a name synonymous with the band. Throughout the remainder of that year there were quite a few other things which would, for once and all, put the final nail in The Beatles' touring coffin.

Their first date during that year was a May 1st appearance at the *New Musical Express'* Poll Winners Concert at the Empire Pool, Wembley. It had been so long since their last UK appearance that all the fans were anxious to hear the new songs. If *Rubber Soul* had been anything to go by, they were in for a treat. Assuming, that was, they would perform some of the new material from the current recording sessions. As it turned out there were no new songs in their five-song set. Their short set consisted of recent (1965) songs; two singles, *I Feel Fine* and *Day Tripper*; two *Rubber Soul* album tracks, *Nowhere Man* and *If I Needed Someone;* and one B-side, the stomping rocking *I'm Down*.

The Wembley show was, as it turns out, their final English concert appearance, a prelude to a world tour but their final UK appearance nonetheless.

First stop off on their world tour was Japan, where they were to perform five shows in three days at the hallowed Budokan Hall, starting on June 23rd 1966. So hallowed in fact was the venue that a number of people complained (publicly) about The Beatles being allowed to perform there. It's hard to appreciate in these more liberal times just how difficult and dangerous it was for The Beatles to be in that environment. Basically The Beatles were prisoners in their own hotel, trapped on the eighteenth floor with the lift stopping at the seventeenth. They were rushed in armoured cars to and from the venues and were not allowed out. Traders however, in the name of international commerce, were allowed to visit The Beatles in their hotel rooms to sell their local wares.

So it was all a bit hairy, but that wasn't the really important thing that came out of the Japanese gigs. It just may have been due to the fact that the Japanese where incredibly polite and respectful or, equally, it may have been the 3,000 armed police packed into the Budokan for each Beatles performance, but the audience were incredibly restrained and well mannered. And quiet! And when you have a quiet audience, you create a situation where the band was able to hear themselves. Hear themselves, in fact, for the first time in years and they were very depressed about how bad they sounded. They hadn't realised they'd become quite so sloppy; out of key, out of time and maybe even out of song. Strike one.

Strike two came when they visited the Philippines on their final world tour. We all know now about what Imelda Marcos and her husband were up to but back then they were succeeding at convincing the world that they were well loved (wannabe) royals who had the support of their nation. Imelda announced to the press that she would be attending The Beatles' concerts and that The Beatles, in return, would be attending the palace to have tea and biscuits with her and her friends. The only problem was that everyone neglected to inform The Beatles about these arrangements and about the fact that their carriage had arrived.

Brian Epstein refused to wake his charges from their well-earned slumber. Imelda proved she was not one to be humiliated in public, particularly in front of her friends. The old palace press machine sprang into action, whipping up a storm among the public. There were riots and protests and a whole hullabaloo. The Beatles' security was withdrawn. The promoter of the concert at The Rizal Memorial Football Stadium, Manila (he who had neglected to advise The Beatles about their audience with her royal shoe-ness) is a gentleman, a Mr. Ramon Ramos, whose name bears repeating here just in case you should ever meet him. Mr Ramon Ramos refused to pay Brian Epstein the vast funds due to The Beatles for fulfilling their side of the contract and selling 80,000 tickets over two shows on the one day.

And there's more. The tax authorities contacted Epstein and informed him that they would not be able to leave the country until he paid income tax on their sizeable fee. The same authorities were not interested in small technicalities, such as the fact that The Beatles hadn't yet been paid the fee, nor were they likely to be, even though the contract with the promoter called for said promoter to pay any and all taxes. This bribe - sorry, did I say bribe? Of course I meant *tax* - Brian Epstein eventually paid this tax and he organised a TV interview from his hotel to tell The Beatles' fans the Liverpool side of the story.

Unfortunately the country was hit by a freak electrical interference for the entire (exact) time Brian Epstein was on TV and The Beatles' story was never heard. Surprisingly (surprising that is if you were a monk in the Himalayas) the electrical interference disappeared as quickly as it had arrived, the very second Brian finished on air!

The Beatles, still under siege in the hotel, eventually managed to make a run for it, minus security, to the airport. They were caught by an unruly crowd who manhandled them and in the scuffle several of The Beatles' party were hurt. Brian Epstein was thrown to the floor and sprained his ankle. They had been advised that they would be shot at as they made their way to the aeroplane and literally had to run the gauntlet for their lives. But their ordeal was not over yet. The authorities advised them that when their plane had landed, a few days earlier, the proper paperwork had not been completed and so, as they had not yet officially entered the country, they surely couldn't possibly leave it. There was a tense hour while Mal Evans and Derek Taylor returned to the airport to (successfully) negotiate their release.

As the plane was taxiing up the runway, Epstein would not have been winning any popularity competitions. He was bearing the brunt for the entire incident. As I've already mentioned, this was strike two and a very bad strike at that, as bad as you could get. For a few years now The Beatles had been subject to such behind-the-scenes treatment. Obviously nowhere as bad the Philippines experience. The fans were fine and kept their distance and were satisfied with the music but officials, politicians, dignitaries, police chiefs, etc all wanted their own little piece of The Beatles.

I'm sure you know the game; three strikes and you're out. Perhaps the biggest strike was just around the corner. Earlier in the year, in London, John Lennon had been giving an interview to a friend of his, Maureen Cleave of the London *Evening Standard*. John had been studying religion recently and in the course of the interview he alluded to the fact that he thought Christianity was on the way out (a fact) and that The Beatles were more popular than Christianity (a fact). This was all very well in the current love culture of liberal England but some of the Bible thumpers in the US of A took exception to it.

The problem with churches is that although their popularity *was* on the wane, they were very powerful. Soon, public record-burning sessions were going on all over America, organised and promoted by radio stations in several God-fearing states. Some radio stations even chose to ban playing Beatles records. It's worth pointing out here that a number of those pious stations had never played, nor where they likely to play, Beatles music in the first place. But a bandwagon is, as we all know, a very savoury gravy train.

Also, it is interesting to note that the record shops in these bonfire areas were doing an amazing trade in Beatles records prior to the local torchings. It even appeared that God was taking part in the debate because a certain station, a Radio Klue in Longview Texas, was struck by lightning. It struck the day after the station organised their particular record-burning session. The flash from the heavens not only burnt out the transmitter, closing the station down, but it also stuck the news editor, leaving him wishing he'd wore his brown trousers on that particular morning.

Needless to say, with all these nutters running riot, the tour was fraught with incidents. The most frightening of these probably took place in the Memphis Coliseum on 19th August 1966 when six local Ku Klux Klan members threw rubbish at The Beatles on stage as they performed. Someone also threw a firecracker on stage during the performance and the band instinctively looked from one to each other to see which of them had been shot. In spite of all of this, the true measure of the fans' feeling at this time was demonstrated by the fact that *Revolver* was number one in the charts and showed no sign of slipping.

By the time The Beatles reached their final date on the American tour at Candlestick Park in San Francisco, on 29th August 1966, they had already decided it was to be the final gig, not just of an event-ridden tour but also of their career. Yes, a sad day for Beatles fans, very sad in fact, but none of us would have wished them the lives they were being forced to tread. More importantly if they hadn't taken such a drastic decision, their music would most definitely have suffered. It's hard today to realise exactly what such a decision meant, or potentially could have meant to their career. Then, in the sixties, touring was everything. Touring *was* the career. Turning their back on touring could have meant the end of The Beatles. At this point however, the musicians were so fried by it all, that to end the touring was their only option.

Strike three and out!

Brian Epstein was devastated and heartbroken by their decision. He knew in a way it meant less involvement from him in their careers. The boys made the music; he looked after the concerts and television appearances, both of which now would be non-existent. Epstein twice attempted suicide in 1966. Had this been a call for help? Was his personal life a mess? Had he been unable to fill the dramatic void in his life by the shift in The Beatles' priorities? Who knows? But whatever it was, obviously he'd been unable to achieve anywhere near the fulfilment from the host of other artists he represented than he had from The Beatles. There was talk of deals going wrong and all that, but I think it was all idle gossip from those jealous who hadn't been involved with The Beatles, and, as I mentioned before, he was *the* first pop group manager. He paved the way others are still following. He was efficient and honest. He shared the vision, had tremendous flair and was a brave tactician with class - loads of class.

After the American nightmare, and maybe even as a result of it, The Beatles started to work on a project that would make every other songwriter in England, with the possible exception of Ray Davies, want to pack up writing forever.

The Beatles ended 1966 with touring forever a thing of the past. Following a sabbatical which afforded John the time to act in the Dick Lester-directed film, *How I Won The War*, George visited India for six weeks, during which time he studied Yoga, Indian culture in general, and the sitar in particular. Paul (along with George Martin) composed and recorded the soundtrack music for the film, *The Family Way*, and Ringo, more chilled than the others, did not feel any need to fill the space, and enjoyed a well-earned rest. Suitably refreshed, they, along with producer George Martin and engineer Geoff Emerick, regrouped at Abbey Road studios on Thursday 24th November 1966 to commence work on what is arguably the most famous album ever released. In it's own way *Sergeant Pepper's Lonely Hearts Club Band* is proving to be as popular and enduring as any of the works by accepted greats such as Beethoven, Mozart or Bach.

For the first time The Beatles were not under any delivery date pressure. Epstein had already advised EMI that there was no chance the new album would be released in time for the extremely lucrative Christmas market. The EMI bods ensured their bonuses by putting together the *Oldies But Goldies* compilation album and shipping it in time for the Christmas rush. The one good thing about *Oldies But Goldies* was that it, with the inclusion of the track *Bad Boy*, brought the UK and USA up to date with each other for the first time. The Americans, remember the capital people at Capitol who didn't want to put The Beatles' music out in the first place, well they were releasing an average of three US Beatles albums for every two albums released by The Beatles in the UK. They achieved this by culling tracks from various albums, singles and EP's to create their own additional releases. Brian Epstein was negotiating a new contract with EMI. The contract, which was eventually signed in January 1967, tied John, Paul, George and Ringo up to EMI, as members of The Beatles and as solo artists for the following nine years. Needless to say, The Beatles were to enjoy a greatly increased record royalty rate and an assurance that all future worldwide releases would be identical to the official UK releases.

For the first time they had no pressures to work under or deadlines to work to. In a way, this time in the studio was as much for The Beatles to see if, creatively speaking, they could exist as a studio identity as well as (hopefully for EMI and the rest of us) producing a new album. Towards the end of the touring, all four Beatles hated the live arena, although it did give them a natural base and a basic need to stay together. Paul was the last to admit this. It should be said here that they really were very lucky to escape the touring experience with their lives, not to mention their sanity, and it speaks volumes for them as humans that they did in fact escape with the latter, firmly intact.

They were no longer the mop tops, singing comforting songs about boys and girls and lost love. They collectively grew their hair, beards and/ or, moustaches. The identical suits had gone by the wayside replaced by casual, colourful, vibrant clothes. Gone were the painfully youthful looks of George and Paul. The craziness had made them all older (naturally), more experienced (definitely), and wiser (noticeably). Yes, wiser... but still human. Their experimentation with drugs was opening their minds and, creatively speaking, inspiring them on different levels. Invariably though they would have to re-record music recorded while under the influence, no matter how great they thought it had sounded at the time.

Now they were all gathered together in Abbey Road Studios, London NW1, to create music which, for first time in their career, they would not have to attempt to perform live. They had an open canvas upon which to paint their weird and wonderful new pictures, drawing from a full palette of colours they hadn't even known existed five years previously. There were no restrictions, excepting the four-track recording machine. One of the things I still find incredible about *Sgt Pepper's* is how they managed to make an album so rich and textured using only a four track recording machine. Admittedly they had magicians, George Martin and engineer Geoff Emerick, continuously mixing down the tracks to free up space for the ever increasing wave of ideas thrown at them by the four principals.

How it works is this. Say you record a four-piece string section. To give each of the instruments clarity, you record each on their own track. Then, when you complete the recording, you mix them all down to sympathetic levels in relationship to each other on to one track, freeing up the remaining three. Now it sounds quite simple when you put it like that, but at the same time you are mixing down, you have to try and look into the future and see what else you, or The Beatles, may wish to add so you leave enough space in the audio picture for such eventualities. George Martin was the master in this area and he and Geoff Emerick were able to deal with every eventuality thrown at them. Necessity *is* the mother of invention, and it was probably during these sessions that people started to dream of eight track machines or sixteen track machines or even, going for broke, 'How about a thirty-two track machine?' Today, even the thirty-two track jobbies can be slaved up to produce ... well basically whatever you need, in multiples of thirty-two.

But in all of this, the funny thing was, I think, that even if they had an eight, sixteen or thirty two track recording machine, instead of the standard four track, I doubt *Sgt Pepper's* could have turned out any better an album than the one it is. Of the several Grammys (record industry's Oscars) *Sgt Pepper's* won, there were none more deserving than the one presented to Geoff Emerick for Best Engineering.

I mentioned at the beginning of this chapter about *Sgt Pepper's* proving to be as popular and as lasting as some of the great classical composers. I didn't mean I felt it was *better* than any of their works, because I feel that would be as stupid as saying one of those Greats' works was better than the others. No, I meant that The Beatles had put something, a work, out there into the world and the world had reacted to it and adopted it for now and forever. But like the classical composers, Liverpool's finest, ably aided and abetted by George Martin, were creating sound pictures, using everything available to them. Unlike the Greats they were using voice, natural traditional instruments and unnatural (or synthetic) sounds.

In November 1966 the introduction to the first song they recorded, as part of these sessions, was played on an instrument never used before in recording. It was a Mellotron, an electronic instrument - the forerunner to the synthesizer - that used pre-recorded tapes. These tapes were activated by the use of a keyboard, creating an electronic version of strings, brass, voice, anything really that you chose to pre-record. In the case of the song in question, the classic *Strawberry Fields Forever*, they used it to 'recreate' a flute sound. This was a song written by a homesick John when he was on the set of the film, *How I Won the War*. *Strawberry Fields Forever* is a song about John's long lost Liverpool. It is the Beatles song he was often quoted as saying was his finest moment. Strawberry Fields is a neighbourhood John lived in for a time and usually you have to leave a place to discover its real beauty. This is exactly what John Lennon was doing in this song. He was far away in Spain working on the film set and although Neil Aspinall was permanently with him on the set and Ringo came to visit he was still obviously thinking a lot about back home.

John writes a song, the ground breaking *Strawberry Fields Forever*, about Liverpool, which prompts Paul to write a song about Liverpool, *Penny Lane*. Both were totally different. John's lyrics were surreal and ambient, Paul's lyrics, real and, as usual, very visual. Paul, as with *Eleanor Rigby*, created a socially observant mini-movie with believable (perhaps even real) characters, all set around Liverpool 18, and a day in the life of the famous barber's shop, Bioletti's. 'In Penny Lane the barber shaves another customer' Paul sings and immediately you're right in there with him and pretty soon you're off on this wonderful trip. And you know what? Both songs compliment each other. Both are written by the best writers around and show in their diversity, the magic of The Beatles. These songs were like chalk and cheese - one an electronic production and the other a very clean recording of natural instruments - but in a way, they sat together as comfortably as Laurel and Hardy on a big sofa.

They worked so well together that EMI, anxious for a single, nicked both the songs, which at that point were meant to have been the first two songs on a concept album about Liverpool, and rushed them out as a double A-sided single (The Beatles' third). In a way it's ironic, not to mention sad, that it should have been this single, perhaps one of the best singles ever released, that would be the first single since The Beatles hit the top with *Please Please Me*, which didn't reach number one in the UK charts. Sadly it peaked at number two. It would have been their thirteenth number one, so perhaps part of the secret of the chart failure lies there. *Could* it really have failed to make the number one position just because it would have been their thirteenth No. 1 single? The Beatles made yet another innovative video clip for their two tracks. Groundbreaking again, in that this was not a performance piece by the band but in fact a very surreal film, with the running, jumping and spooky Beatles. John Lennon wearing in public, for the first time, the glasses he'd been wearing for so long in private. In the sixties glasses and wives were bad for the image and so both were kept (equally) in the background. This made for strained relationships and strained book reading.

It's all over, the critics cried. They're finished. My dad told me, when talking about others in public always use only the sweetest of words. 'You may have to eat them someday,' he'd remind me. Well the critics' words were anything but sweet, but if the excitement generated up on Abbey

Road Studios was anything to go by, the critics were all going to be sitting down to an unwanted feast six months later.

Sergeant Pepper's Lonely Heart's Club Band was always meant to be a concept album or a theme album of some sort; of that there is no question. Some of the rumours around Liverpool at the time were that it was in fact meant to be an album with songs about Liverpool. The third song they recorded was *When I'm Sixty Four*, a Paul McCartney vaudeville, Indigo Jolliphant-type song that they had been performing (during equipment breakdowns) as early as the Cavern days. Now Paul's Dad had just celebrated his sixty-fourth birthday and so it was duly dragged out and recorded for the Liverpool album. Then EMI released *Strawberry Fields Forever* and *Penny Lane* and as The Beatles didn't like fans having to buy their songs twice (as singles and album tracks) they withdrew those two pivotal songs from the album's short list.

In times of trouble you could always leave it to Paul to come up with an idea or, as on this occasion, a concept. And he did.

The San Francisco scene was just starting up and all the bands over there had weird and wonderful names like Big Brother and the Holding Company, Grace Slick and The Jefferson Airplane and a few cods had even put a group together called Country Joe and The Fish. Inspired by these names, Paul suggested, and the other's agreed, making up a fictitious band and having the album be the showpiece of this imaginary band. Make it a real show so that the show could go out on tour and they could all stay at home. Great idea. What would they call the band? *Sergeant Pepper's Lonely Hearts Club Band* of course. So they did, and the rest as they say... was 90% perspiration.

The title track shows The Beatles to be a group as tight and as rocking as any other band out there. It's also a very exciting track that actually entices you into the show. The whole project was gathering steam at this point and cameras were recording their every studio move for a possible television special. The other revolutionary idea they came up with was to segue the songs into another. It was a show, after all, and there was no need or reason for disruptive breaks. *Sgt Pepper's* (the song) melted into the next track, with audience noise (this actually lifted from The Beatles in concert at the Hollywood Bowl), so effectively that you couldn't see the join. The next song was *With A Little Help From My Friends,* written for and about Ringo (we assume). Ringo took on the character name, Billy Shears, for his place in the band.

There, sadly, the original idea ran out of steam. The remaining songs, except for the reprise of *Sgt Pepper's Lonely Heart Club Band*, have no link to the original concept. They were all exceptional but in no way connected, except in that they all shared a show-cum-circus kind of feel.

A Day In The Life is a Beatles masterpiece in anyone's book and displays some of the most soulful singing ever performed by John Lennon. It shows the collective genius of the Lennon & McCartney writing team. John took his inspiration from two newspaper stories. First there was Tara Browne, a friend and one of the Guinness heirs, who had been killed in a car crash, and secondly there was a story about how many holes there were in Blackburn, Lancashire. There was a natural gap in the middle of John's song and he, at the time of the original recording, didn't know what he was going to put in. So they recorded the song, leaving a gap with the dependable Mal Evans counting 24 bars and setting off an alarm clock at the end of the break so everyone would know when to start playing again.

So, John had a beginning and an end to a song but he didn't know what to do in the middle. Paul McCartney, on the other hand, had this little bit of a song, you know some he'd probably add to or finish off some day. But why not use that for the middle of John's song? Why not indeed, so they did. Now at least they had the foundation for the song. That was one of the good things about The Beatles in the studio. They would always go with the best idea for a track, no matter who suggested it; there was none of 'It's my song and I want....' That was for later, when there was no Beatles.

Because Paul sang *I'd Love To Turn You On* during his section of *A Day In The Life*, the BBC was to ban the song from airplay as they did another song on this album, effectively causing the projected television recording of the making of the album to be doomed to the shelves.

One of the things they did record for television and keep was the orchestra recording their contribution for inclusion on this track. The Beatles wanted an orgasmic orchestral climax on the end of the recording of *A Day In The Life*. They wanted all the instruments to start on their lowest (deepest) note and work their way up into a frenzied crescendo as the musicians all hit their highest note simultaneously. The Beatles asked the orchestra, all forty of them, to dress up in dinner jackets, but also to wear something silly to add to the party atmosphere at the recording. They also invited some of their friends and so, people like Mick Jagger were to be filmed sitting around at The Beatles' feet during this historic recording.

Mal Evans and Neil Aspinall were still just as invaluable to The Beatles. I'd imagine they thought that the end of the gigging would also be the end of their career with The Beatles. Not so. They were needed just as much in the studio as they were on the road. They were trusted members of the community at a time when trust was worth more than its weight in gold. In order to achieve the BIG piano note (E Major) which concluded *A Day In The Life*, John, Paul, Ringo and Mal had all to hit *the* note simultaneously on separate pianos, while George Martin added weight on the harmonium.

Now they had the beginning and the end to their album. All they had to do was fill in the middle bits. *Good Morning Good Morning* is a John song and inspired by a Kellogg's TV advert with the Sounds Incorporate lending their brass section. The Sounds Incorporate were the top instrumental unit of the day and frequently toured as a back-up band for American soul artists touring the UK without their bands. They were also managed by Brian Epstein and occasionally toured as an opening act for The Beatles.

The Beatles originally recorded *Only A Northern Song* as George Harrison's composition for *Sgt. Pepper's*, but probably because they were never able to do justice to the song it didn't make the cut and didn't in fact resurface until the *Yellow Submarine* album a few years later. George did, however, with help from his Indian friends (there were no other Beatles on the recording session) record *Within You Without You*. This, as you well know, did make the historic album.

Fixing A Hole apparently was the easiest song on the album to record on this great idea. But they were getting their ideas from everywhere. John Lennon bought an old circus poster, advertising a circus appearance in Rochdale in February 1843 and pulled all the performers mentioned on the poster into a song, as you do, called *Being For The Benefit Of Mr Kite*. George Martin, under instructions to come up with something 'fairgroundy' and 'circusy', secured library sounds of the same, cut the tapes up into little pieces, threw the fragments into the air, picked them up from the floor and stuck them all back together again to create a bizarre sonic miss-mash. Then he added some of his own harmonium playing to the song, completing yet another unconnected scene in the magical show.

If George Martin was happy with his work on *Mr Kite,* he was distinctly unhappy to discover that an impatient Paul had decided, rather than wait for his producer to return from a function, he would hire Mike Leander to do a string arrangement for his song, *She's Leaving Home.* It was the first time strings were to be included on a Beatle record which were not arranged by George Martin. The arrangement is good, although somewhat more predictable than George Martin's adventurous arrangements, and the recording of this song was completed simply with only John and Paul on vocals. It was yet another of Paul's story-in-a-song songs and very effective at that.

Lovely Rita, Getting Better and *Lucy in The Sky With Diamonds* completed the songs for the album. *Lucy* was the second track to be banned by the BBC. The title was not in fact about the drug LSD (*L*ucy/*S*ky/*D*iamonds) but was John's son Julian's description of a painting he had brought home from school. Again, with *Getting Better,* we see the alternative sides of The Beatles, with positive Paul singing, 'It's Getting Better all the Time' (referring to his progress with learning to drive) and dour John countering with, 'It can't get much worse.'

All good stuff, and they had the album completed. Apart from one little addition, that was. The final recording for *Sergeant Pepper's Lonely Heart Club Band* was carried out on Friday 21st April 1967 when they recorded a high pitched fifteen kilocycle whistle, a noise only dogs could hear, which was placed just after the aforementioned single (multi-tracked) E Major piano note which was to fade forever and forever.

Over five months, The Beatles spent a staggering seven hundred hours working on their masterwork. A long time in those days, but these days probably about the time it would take the Spinal Tap-type drummers to get their drum sound correct. Back then however, EMI owned the studio and none of the recording costs were billed to the artist. Was it around that time that record company's accountants considered starting to bill the band for their studio time?

The sleeve of this album is possibly the most famous album sleeve in the world. It was Paul McCartney's idea, although some of the people he hired to do pieces of the work on it would later claim credit. It was the first record sleeve to contain printed lyrics. Brian Epstein was so worried about the sleeve that at one point he suggested it might be an idea to release it in a brown paper bag so as not to offend. In the cast of characters adorning the sleeve John Lennon wanted to include Hitler and Jesus. EMI refused and further requested that Gandhi also be removed. Neil and Mal went around all the libraries collecting prints of the various celebrities and a genuine fairground painter, Joseph Ephrgave, painted the famous drumhead. I wonder where that is now? Who has the Sergeant Pepper drum head?

Sergeant Pepper's Lonely Hearts Club Band (or PCS 7027 as it was known to EMI's accountants) was released on 1st June 1967), significantly enough, in the year of the summer of Love (the capital L is intentional). The pirate radio station, Radio London, played the album in its entirety on the air, claiming a first for both themselves and The Beatles. In England, with presales of a quarter of a million copies, *Sgt Pepper's* shot straight to the top of the charts, where it remained for twenty weeks, dropped to the number two position for eleven weeks and then returned to the top during the first week of 1968 for a further two weeks.

It is the biggest selling UK album ever! That is by anyone before or since. With sales now approaching a staggering four and a half million copies. Around the time of the release of *Sgt Pepper's*, EMI announced that The Beatles had sold (across all their records and counting each album as six unit sales, and a single as one unit) 200 million units!

I think it is interesting to note the top ten records (singles) the week *Sgt. Pepper's* was released.

1. The Tremeloes	Silence is Golden
2. The Kinks.	Waterloo Sunset
3. The Mamas & The Papas.	Dedicated to the One I Love
4. Procol Harum	A Whiter Shade of Pale
5. Beach Boys	Then I Kissed Her
6. Jimi Hendrix Experience	The Wind Cries Mary
7. Engelbert Humperdinck	There Goes my Everything
8. Supremes	The Happening
9. The Who	Pictures of Lily
10. Dubliners	Seven Drunken Nights.

Equally interesting to note, the number two single was written by Ray Davies, who, with his consistency and insightful songs, was proving to be the best English songwriter who didn't come for Liverpool and wasn't a member of The Beatles.

In America, with pre-sales of over a million copies *Sgt Pepper's* went straight to number one and remained in the charts for over two years. It has now sold over twelve million copies in America. At this point, worldwide sales must be approaching the thirty million mark for this phenomenally successful album.

During the summer of 1967 I was living in Northern Ireland, getting ready to leave for London in fact. I'd bought the record the day it was released but hadn't had a chance to listen to it too much, preoccupied as I then was with trying to get gigs for my first group, The Blues By Five. But I had liked the album, liked it a lot. Then, one Saturday evening, I was at this party in Cookstown, Co. Tyrone and it was in some church hall. All the walls were covered with colourful posters and streamers and coloured balloons were hanging about everywhere and the music was great and as they say over there, the craic was ninety. People were talking, laughing, joking and dancing. Some were sitting around, drinking and having a good time and then someone put *Sergeant Pepper's Lonely Hearts Club Band* on the PA system.

One by one the party people stopped talking and chatting and the noise and bustle of the party died down completely until the entire party was being seduced by this beautiful and inspiring music. People were smiling and loving it and happiness was spreading from one to another with the same power and speed panic can move through a gathering. Every new track drew everyone in deeper and deeper into this new world. Our new world, a world created for us by The Beatles. It was like everything they had ever done had been leading up to that point. Every note of music they had ever played; every song they had ever composed had been in preparation for this moment, the moment they captured with *Sergeant Pepper's Lonely Hearts Club Band*. It didn't matter that perhaps the *Revolver* album might have been a better album. It didn't matter that touring had nearly destroyed the our band. It didn't matter that I didn't have someone there with me to love and share this with; there was already more than enough love in the air. And all of it created by The Beatles. All that mattered was that they had fulfilled their promise. This album wasn't a great album because it sold lots of copies. The album sold lots of copies, purely and simply, because it was a great album. Maybe even the perfect album.

And the thing about the party that night in Cookstown was that we were all sharing it, sharing the pleasure. And as it was being shared, the pleasure grew. When John Lennon started to sing *A Day In the Life,* I swear to you I felt shivers run down my spine, the hairs on the back of my neck stood up and my throat went dry. I could feel my nostrils tightening as though tears were going to flow. Not one person felt any different, I bet you. No one moved a muscle for fear of spoiling the mood. As the last note, the E Major, drifted into silence, everyone was left stunned and speechless. It was like a mass turn-on but instead of the buzz being incited by a drug, it had been induced by the show The Beatles had wanted to present to us, possibly for years. The show they knew they could never do on stage but felt they could do by sending it out to us in the form of the *Sergeant Pepper's Lonely Hearts Club Band* album. I know that probably sounds as if I may have been indulging in some of the harmful chemicals I alluded to. I wasn't, I never have and I never will. I've never felt the need to. But you really had to be there, in Cookstown on that spectacular summer evening, to know what I'm on about. It was a perfect moment. One of those moments that rarely appear in your life but when they do you have to try and find some way to savour them and protect them in your memory. All I can tell you is that as we strained to hear the disappearing E Major, there was the most incredible feeling of elation. Everyone clapped their hands, we didn't know what else to do. We just clapped and clapped and then clapped some more.

You'll probably never ever meet anyone who can tell you what it was like the first time the 1812 Overture was performed, or what it was like sitting in the Olympia Theatre in Dublin when The Hallelujah Chorus was receiving its world premier. In fact, I can guarantee you won't. Time has drawn a line under both of those. But I'm happy to tell you with hand on heart that for me what they felt could not have compared with the experience I felt while listening to The Beatles' masterwork

It was never the same. I never ever experienced that buzz again. I don't tell you that with the slightest regret. I am proud to have been alive in that time and enjoyed that once in a lifetime experience. I still love and enjoy listening to the record. But it just may have been the communal spirit between all at the party that summer evening in Cookstown, and probably subconsciously acknowledging that similar parties were going on the length and breadth of Ireland and England, and I suppose for an experience to have been so special meant that it certainly wasn't going to be an experience which could be repeated frequently, if ever.

And it all came from the music, the music of The Beatles.

8: The Beatles?
Three Hundred Thousand, Eight Hundred and One.

It is fitting that during this summer, the Summer of Love, The Beatles, having reached their artistic and commercial peak, should have been involved in a project which took them live into 350,000,000 homes over five continents.

The Beatles, as the most famous group ever, were commissioned to write a piece of music, as England's official representatives, to launch the live television link-up via satellite in a BBC programme called *Our World*. In those days, it was a big thing. Television was still considered to be the wireless in the corner, which occasionally showed distorted pictures. It had yet to reach the stage were it controlled all domestic life - that is all domestic life, as we know it.

The Beatles being The Beatles, and never ones to shirk from a challenge, decided they would do their section live and the live recording would be the official single. John Lennon wrote the song. The backing tracks were rehearsed and recorded at the Olympic Studio in Barnes. On the designated day, 25th June 1967, The Beatles assembled with friends, musicians and the ever-present cameras. The studio was decorated in multi-coloured streamers, banners and balloons. The Beatles themselves were dressed to the nines in their new flamboyant hippie gear. Among those present were girlfriends and wives, Donovan, Marianne Faithfull, Mike Love and Mick Jagger, caught on camera sitting at John Lennon's feet. Mr. Jagger seemed to spend quite a bit of the sixties sitting at The Beatles' feet, a position from which he seemed then, or even now, to be unable to rise from.

The message John and his fellow travellers, of the mind and globe, had come up with, was *All You Need Is Love*. It was probably more of a chant than a song, but a very infectious chant and one with a message. A message, which if, had it been taken to heart, would have made the world a much better place. But even then there were darker powers lurking around the corner.

The live on air *All You Need Is Love* was produced by the ever trusted and inventive George Martin and released as a single with *Baby You're A Rich Man* on the B-side (Parlophone Records, released on Friday 7th July 1967). *Baby You're a Rich Man* might have been written about a trip The Beatles took to Greece that summer. The intention was to buy an island

and for The Beatles and their friends to retreat to and form a commune. They lorded it up for a week or so on expensive yachts and in exclusive villas and returned to the UK, not having made the purchase but (via Paul's pen) with the B-side of their next single.

The rumours of The Beatles' imminent demise when *Strawberry Fields Forever/Penny Lane* failed to reach number one in the chart was proven to be premature as *All You Need Is Love* shot to the top of the charts and remained there for three weeks.

In the middle of all this, The Beatles had already commenced work on their next project, yet another Paul idea. The recording part of this project took place a matter of only five days after they completed work on the monumental *Sgt. Pepper's* recording session. The new project was *The Magical Mystery Tour*. The idea (very hippie) was that they were to get on a bus with a few friends, bring along a few crates of beer and a few shovels full of spaghetti, and travel around having a laugh and recording it all for a film.

Humour was a big thing in The Beatles' camp. They had a great ability to laugh at things, including, it must be noted, themselves. The Beatles frequently portrayed the fun side of life in their music. The main difference (apart from the quality of the music that was) between them and, say, the Stones, for instance, was, quite simply, a sense of humour. I always put that down to the Liverpudlian influence.

They also discovered that summer, via George Harrison, the teaching of Maharishi Mahesh Yogi. Basically the Maharishi taught those who would listen that one could achieve spiritual enlightenment through Transcendental Meditation. Ten minutes in the morning and ten minutes in the evening was all that was required to transport you to another level of contentment. Towards the end of August 1967, The Beatles and entourage boarded a train at St Pancras for Bangor in Wales to take instruction in meditation.

Sadly, very sadly, while The Beatles were in Bangor, Brian Epstein accidentally took an overdose of pills.

Their mentor, manager, partner and friend was dead.

Brian Epstein was thirty-two years old when he died. Some say he was unhappy. He was reportedly very unhappy in his personal life and let's not forget that we're talking about the not-so-liberal sixties. He was also unhappy in his business life. The Beatles, the musical force that he helped bring to the world, had decided to give up touring. And that had always been his big thing, organising and plotting their rise through concerts, films and media promotion. He had succeeded brilliantly in his endeavours and, as I keep saying, he paved the way for every manager who was to follow.

But when The Beatles had, in effect, retired from the road, they were eagerly jumping to the next phase of their career and as a result, at least on paper, there would have been less need for a manager. But I think Brian would have reinvented his role as The Beatles' manager just as The Beatles were very successfully and creatively reinventing the band. He'd been depressed; he'd been given some anti-depressant pills. Sadly, when mixed with alcohol they proved to be lethal. Such was also the case with several other celebrities, all of whom, at some stage, were accused of committing suicide. But I would like to think that people like Mama Cass, Keith Moon, Jimi Hendrix, Jim Morrison and Brian Epstein, all talented young people in their prime, were guilty of nothing more than mixing their medication with alcohol, a human mistake, which sadly proved to be fatal.

That's *my* personal view. I'm quite sure that this same story, told even by any of the four principals involved, would be different. Yes, I'm sure those individual accounts would be totally different from each other, not to mention my perspective.

On camera afterwards John, Paul, George & Ringo all looked devastated, looked like they were in shock. I've never been able to get my head around the concept of journalists or television crews feeling the need to stick a microphone in the face of a recently bereaved celebrity and asking them how they feel. You'd think the media should know by now it takes you years to work out how you feel. There was no doubt that the death of Brian Epstein left a huge void in The Beatles' lives. A void they tried to fill immediately by heading off to India to study further with the Maharishi. The funniest story I remember reading about that trip was the one where his great holiness was getting a bit frisky with one of the actresses and The Beatles were annoyed by his actions. Mr Yogi asked them why they were so upset and John Lennon replied that if he were indeed as spiritual as he was claiming, he'd know exactly what was on their mind.

It was also during this visit that John, Paul and George undertook a lot of individual song writing. These songs were to be the creative nucleus of the double album called *The Beatles*, aka *The White Album*, because of its unblemished cover. The sole marking on the cover was an embossed 'The Beatles' and an individual number. Each album was stamped with its own number making each copy unique. I wonder who had copies numbered 1, 2, 3 and 4. Ringo, supposedly, had one of the several number fives in circulation. I know I had copy number 0300801; I still do in fact. *The White Album* does have its moments, like the incredible *While My Guitar Gently Weeps*, George at his best, aided and abetted by his mate Eric Clapton on guitar. This was a very rare occasion of an outside musician playing on a Beatles record. Eric Clapton celebrated the occasion by giving George the Les Paul Guitar he used for the guitar solo on the track. George thought it was a beautiful guitar and it remained one of his favourites.

George for his part had started to concentrate on his guitar playing once again. Some say the main reason George, during the period, became a great guitar player was because he realized that he would never ever be a great sitar player but he felt that if he applied himself to the guitar he might become great at that. It seems a pathetic understatement to say that George Harrison did become a great guitarist. I've met so many musicians, particularly American, who started off playing mainly due to George's inspirational work. People like Jeff Lyne have gone on record as saying that George was one of the best slide guitar players in the world.

The White Album contained some gems like *Ob La Di, Ob La Da,* very poppy, another favourite for kids of all ages and introducing West Indian influenced music to a wider audience, *Birthday*, very heavy and along with *Helter Skelter* and *Yer Blues*, perhaps the beginnings of Heavy Rock and Heavy Metal music. *Yer Blues* in particular shows just how tight The Beatles had become again. When you have a band, a great band, and they are all playing well together the sound they collectively create is one of the rare occasions when result is greater than the sum total of the parts. Very few bands reach this telepathic point. I'd say The Beatles definitely were one of these bands and I'd also include Rockpile, Creedence Clearwater Revival, The Blue Nile, Genesis (with Peter Gabriel) and The Undertones, all bands where the musicians give themselves (their individuality) up to the benefit of the band sound.

The Beach Boys-influenced *Back In The USSR* sets the record off to a joyous, uplifting, in your face, start. On the other hand, the confused and pointless art piece *Revolution No 9,* very nearly ground the album to a halt completely. There was enough material on this album that they could easily have dropped this experimental indulgence.

It doesn't matter that *The White Album* could, or should, have been a single album as George Martin suggests. That it could have made a brilliant single album with all the fat cut off it. What matters is that it's The Beatles flexing their muscles, their new independent individual muscles. At one point during the recording sessions, John, Paul and George were all in separate studios simultaneously working on their own songs. That probably accounts for the variety on the album.

It wasn't enough for The Beatles to want to remake *Rubber Soul* or *Revolver* or *Sgt Pepper's*, brilliant as those albums certainly are. The Beatles preferred, and needed, to head off into uncharted waters rather than paddle around in a familiar pool the way other groups had done. ABBA made a career out of playing at being The Beatles and The Moody Blues, for instance, spent their entire career trying (unsuccessfully) to get their version of *Sgt Pepper's* correct. Electric Light Orchestra, responsible for some of the best 'Beatles' albums never recorded, used *Abbey Road* as their template. But The Beatles were different. They had to play on. They had to move on with what little life there was left in the band. So, taken in this context, *The White Album* can most simply be described as an album The Beatles just had to make. It was a case of 'Hang on there for a minute and we'll be right back with you.'

Or, as Paul McCartney very succinctly put it, 'It's great. It Sold. It's the bloody Beatles' *White Album*, shut up!'

It was the first album to be released on The Beatles' own record label, Apple, and it shot to the top of the charts all over the world, becoming the biggest selling double album by quickly notching up sales in excess of six million

It was during the making of *The White Album* that Ringo Starr left The Beatles. He said he felt unloved, unwanted and unworthy as a musician and a mate. It was probably hardest for Ringo. Being the nice geezer in the band he probably didn't know which way to turn when all his mates, the mates he loved, were all off in separate studios working on their own versions of The Beatles. He must have felt there was nowhere for him to turn.

John, Paul and George realised what was happening and went out of their way to reassure him that there would no Beatles without Ringo. The best band in the world needed the best drummer in the world. It was that simple. And, thankfully, Ringo returned to the fold. Returned, in fact, to a studio decorated from top to bottom with flowers, an outward display of an inward affection organised by his three colleagues.

They were back together again and to some degree enjoying their time in the studio, enjoying their new role as a studio band. The next bit of vinyl available from all good record shops was *Hello Goodbye,* backed by the legendary *I Am The Walrus*. (Parlophone R5655, released 24th November 1967) This was the first of four consecutive Paul songs, specially written as singles. *Hello Goodbye* is an excellent pop song and very commercial but ... few people's favourite, I fear. However, its straight-ahead hook took it straight to the top of the lucrative Christmas charts, where it remained for seven weeks; The Beatles' longest reign at the top since the early days, in fact. It should be noted that George Martin and Brian Epstein's planning was so effective, The Beatles had enjoyed a Christmas number one record every year from 1963 to 1967 (apart from 1966 when there was no Beatles single).

Next came yet another first, the first double EP. Typical really for The Beatles when you think about it; they rarely opted for the easy way out. They had six tracks, too many for a single or an EP and not enough for a full album, so, rather than agreeing to the traditional record company pil-laging and padding it out to a full album, they released a double EP, *Mag-ical Mystery Tour* (Parlophone MMMT-1). It was released on Friday 8th December 1967. The double EP was number two the week *Hello Goodbye* was number one. It featured six good solid Beatles tracks including George's intriguing *Blue Jay Way,* and *Fool On The Hill* was a song all the McCartney impersonators would love to have been able to put their name to.

This was followed quickly with *Lady Madonna* b/w *The Inner Light* (Parlophone R5675, released 15th March 1968). *Lady Madonna* was not one of The Beatles' more popular singles but it did reach number one, where it stayed for two weeks. It was to be The Beatles' last (and four-teenth) single on the Parlophone label. *Lady Madonna's* other distinction is that some people thought it bore more than a passing similarity to Hum-phrey Lyttelton's 1956 Top 20 hit, *Bad Penny Blues,* coincidentally also produced by George Martin. The other strange coincidence was that one of Lyttelton's colleagues, jazz legend Ronnie Scott, led the brass section on the recording of *Lady Madonna.* It would appear the Old Etonian trum-peter didn't come out of the deal too badly; a High Court Judge agreed with him and The Beatles had to pay Mr. Lyttelton a percentage of their royalties. The B-side featured the first appearance on a Beatles single of a George Harrison composition.

When they'd completed some of the recording for *The White Album,* John Lennon wanted *Revolution* (No.1, I hasten to add) to be released as a single. Reportedly he was dissuaded from this on the grounds that it was too slow a track. Quite ironic then that it should be the B-side for the equally slow, but very moving, *Hey Jude* (Apple [Parlophone] R5722, released on Friday 30th August 1968) which was the first single on their own label (even though it still had a Parlophone/EMI number) and the beginning of a concentrated time for The Beatles and Beatles-related material at the top of the singles charts.

John Lennon and his wife Cynthia had broken up and Paul McCartney was on his way to see Cynthia and her son, who shared his dad's troubled looks, probably to console and encourage them (as good friends do). On the car journey Paul had this idea going though his head, 'Hey Jules (for Julian), take a sad song and maker it better.' You know the sentiment, 'Look, it's bad now, I know, but don't worry, it'll get better.'

Paul changed the Jules to Jude because it sounded more country and, pretty soon, had one of the all time classic singles, *Hey Jude*, which, at seven minutes and ten seconds, was the longest single ever to reach number one. With a total of nine weeks, it was to be The Beatles' longest reigning number one single in the US of A, whereas in the UK, although it sold very well, it was knocked from the top spot after only two weeks.

And guess what the offending single was. Mary Hopkins, *Those Were the Days*. Paul McCartney produced Mary Hopkins' first single for The Beatles' Apple label. Paul had previously tried (unsuccessfully) to persuade Denny Laine to record this folksy type song. The next number one single (UK) was from a Sheffield lad called Joe Cocker singing *With A Little Help From My Friends,* a blistering performance on a very original interpretation of the *Sgt Pepper's* song. This classic single was to launch and sustain a career for one of England's best soul singers. No Beatles activity in the charts for a while now as the title song from the Clint Eastwood breakthrough movie, *The Good the Bad and The Ugly,* emerged. However, following this Ennio Morricone-composed song, the Scaffold, a Liverpool co-operative of poets (with a musical bent) featuring Paul McCartney's brother, Mike McGear, reached number one with *Lily The Pink.*

And there's more! The next single to step up to the number one position was The Marmalade with their version of *Ob La Di, Ob La Da*: another Lennon & McCartney number one single. The Beatles had been involved in a project which would produce the single that replaced The Marmalade. We're talking about *Get Back* b/w *Don't Let Me Down* (Apple [Parlophone] R5777, released on Friday 11th April 1969); it came crashing straight into the number one spot of the charts where it enjoyed a six week stay that spring.

As with a lot of the ideas, the one behind the fateful recording sessions for *Get Back* sprang from Paul McCartney. The idea was original, two-fold and, at least on paper, brilliant. Firstly, The Beatles, having invented the term 'studio band', now wanted to *get back* to basics. They wanted to *get back* to playing live together. No over-dubs and no hours and hours working on one small part of a track while poor Ringo would get bored out of his Christmas Tree reading the papers or playing chess. He would normally do his drum part first (so that they could build the song up from the rhythm track, which would invariably consist of drums, bass, guitar - maybe piano - and a guide vocal).

To achieve this feel and yet keep it as a special project involved the second part of Paul's master plan. They would move into a movie studio and rehearse an entire album's worth of new material. The cameras would be present catching The Beatles creating their magic and would also be present when The Beatles performed their first live concert since San Francisco. This concert would consist of The Beatles presenting their new album as they recorded it, both visually and audially. They'd even gone as far as booking the legendary Roundhouse at Chalk Farm, Camden Town, for the concert performance.

They moved into Twickenham Studios for what was sadly to become the winter of their discontent. Instead of capturing The Beatles' magic, the cameras caught the sad disintegration of the group. There were lots of mitigating circumstances. The principals, who'd been together now for nearly ten years, were drifting apart; the studios were cold and not conducive to creating music; the cameras proved to be an intrusion; Yoko was always around - literally never more than a few inches from John; The Beatles had to come in each day at much too early an hour for musicians to be creative, just so they could fit in with the film crews' schedule.

Things came to a head when Paul appeared to provoke George Harrison into an argument over the guitar playing. George appeared too weary of the whole situation to bother to get into the fight. He replied to Paul. 'I'll play whatever you want. I won't play at all, if that's what you want.' It is probably the most dramatic and certainly the saddest line I've ever heard delivered on the silver screen.

Shortly thereafter, George Harrison left the band and the sessions ground to a halt. A few days later they all met up in a pub and agreed that they should *get back* together again and finish the project. They obviously negotiated a better situation and agreed to abandon the coldness of the movie studio for the warmth of their own cosy Apple studios. Alex, their electronic wizard, who in fact wasn't (a wizard), didn't have the studio ready so they brought all the equipment in from outside and had it set up. The Beatles also brought in American Billy Preston on piano and organ to give themselves a much-needed stimulus, not to mention a wee bit of cement.

And they got on with finishing the album. Which as it turns out, apart from a few moments, is a sorry album, and should, in truth, never have been released. I'll hear tracks from the albums around this period, *White Album*, *Let It Be* and *Yellow Submarine*, on the radio or something and I'll go back to them encouraged by that track, but I usually never make it the whole way through the album.

Get Back does however shows them back together as a cracking wee rock group cemented together, as I've said, by Billy Preston, on organ, and shows John Lennon had obviously been spending some time away from Yoko Ono, if only to practice his guitar solos.

The Roundhouse concert never happened. Instead, again for the benefit of the cameras, they performed on top of the Apple Building in Baker Street, stopping the traffic and eventually having their performance stopped by the long arm of the law.

Although the *Get Back* album was the last album to be released, it was not the final album to be recorded. The Beatles, knowing exactly how big a mess the album was, ordered it to be put on the shelves and, although they knew they were going to split up, they decided to get together one more time; this time to do it properly.

9: The Big Wheel Keeps On Turning:
Abbey Road & *Let It Be*

Endings and beginnings, they are the same really aren't they? They inhabit the same space and one begat the other, as John would have said; of course that's St John the Apostle we're talking about. The Beatles' John along with his mates Paul, George and Ringo, sensibly, made the decision not to end The Beatles with *Let it Be,* the name under which *Get Back*, the soundtrack, was eventually released.

The Madchester guru and media man Tony Wilson has this theory that all musical movements last for thirteen years; recent history certainly doesn't contradict him. In The Beatles' case they had done the impossible by singlehandedly becoming a self-contained movement.

Beatlemania, 1957 to 1970.

You'd also have to think that towards the end of the seventies they were well aware of this legacy and their importance in popular music. They were probably even proud and protective of their reputation. There was probably some sort of conscious decision to try and go out on a high, if only to get on with the start of their solo careers with clean slates.

Paul McCartney rang up George Martin and told him that The Beatles would like to return to the studios and make another album. He added that The Beatles would like George Martin to produce them. George Martin agreed, on condition that he was *allowed* to *produce* them. They accepted George's reasonable condition and the sessions took place from July 1st 1969, till the end of August the same year.

Apparently they were happy sessions. Perhaps that was because they'd all agreed and accepted that they were working on *the final* Beatles album. I believe *Let It Be*, the movie and the audio recordings, had left a very bitter taste in their collective mouths.

Abbey Road (Apple [Parlophone] PCs 7088, released on Friday 26th September 1969) on the other hand should have been the album to close their account on. It was The Beatles being The Beatles and being produced by George Martin. The album shows George Harrison with two stunningly beautiful songs, not just Harrison classics, but worthy Beatles classics as well. Frank Sinatra always introduced *Something* (composed by George) as one of the greatest Lennon & McCartney songs. I have to believe his words were carefully chosen. The song *Something* was actually written back while the Fabs were working on *The White Album*. Harrison left the song for six months because he was scared the song was coming together so quickly it might be something else. McCartney said something similar about *Yesterday*. He claimed his evergreen song came to him in a dream - he actually woke up one morning singing the melody.

Here Comes The Sun George wrote while in Eric Clapton's garden. George and Eric were walking around the garden with their guitars, as you do. George was down at Eric's house playing truant from the lawyer meetings at Apple, which always depressed him. George started playing the chord structure of *Here Comes The Sun* and said to Eric, 'Come on, let's write this together?' and Eric said, 'No, that's yours; you've already written it.' The recording of *Here Comes The Sun* is quite exquisite, perhaps one of the perfect Beatle songs with the best acoustic guitar sound ever recorded. There are other great songs on *Abbey Road* as well; songs like *Because* and *The End* with lyrics as profound as anything The Beatles had done. Joe Cocker recorded and had a hit with *She Came In Through The Bathroom Window,* written by Paul McCartney about an incident where a fan broke into his St John's Wood House - the meeting point for The Beatles on their way to the nearby Abbey Road Studios. The Beatles showed off their wonderful blend of voices on *Because*. Once again, out Beach Boying the Beach Boys. It's an incredibly commercial and people-friendly album, a view obviously shared by the record buying public as *Abbey Road* shot straight to the top of the album charts and remained there for 18 weeks. It is the one of Beatles' biggest selling albums, with world-wide sales north of thirty million.

Abbey Road, the album, was sandwiched by two vastly different singles. Before the album came out, John Lennon rushed into the studio with Paul McCartney and the two of them quickly recorded, with Paul taking over Ringo's stool, *The Ballad of John and Yoko*. This was The Beatles' eighteenth, and final, number one single record. The *Ballad of John and Yoko* was backed with a George Harrison tune *Old Brown Shoe* (Apple [Parlophone] R5786, released on Friday 30th May 1969). Shortly after the *Abbey Road* album was shipped, the very melodic *Something* was released. This was the first time in ages that an album track was released as a single. It was issued as their twenty-first single but sadly didn't reach the top, peaking only at number 4. It was the first time one of George Harrison's songs had appeared as the A-side of a Beatles single. The B-side was *Come Together* and the Apple [Parlophone] Records single R5814 was released on 31st October 31st 1969.

The Beatles had been chasing their tails for several years. They wanted to be the best group in Hamburg; accomplished. They wanted to be the best group in Liverpool; likewise, achieved. They wanted to get a record deal; done that, admittedly with a comedy label but nonetheless they had their deal. They wanted to have a number one single; there too they were successful. They wanted to be successful in America; they were, and how! They wanted to be bigger than Elvis. They wanted to make the best albums ever made; they managed this not once, not twice but three, possibly four times.

Don't you see they had to split up to protect their own greatness? When you had all those songs and all those records to your credit where was there left to go? There was absolutely no point in repeating themselves. You'd have to think that they had enough integrity to suss this.

The Beatles had scored a fist of firsts in their short but meteoric career.

First to use feedback.
First to have lyrics on a sleeve.
First to use a gatefold sleeve.
First not to print their name on the sleeve.
First to release an album without the band name on front of sleeve.
First to appear on satellite TV link-up.
First to use pop promotional clips.
First group to appear at an outdoor stadium.
First to have their own record label.
First to use backward recording.
First to use non-musical sounds on recordings.
First to use a Mellotron on a record.
First to have a book dedicated to their lyrics.
First to produce a concept album.
First to develop and use ADT (Automatic Double Tracking) while recording.
First to achieve the top five singles (simultaneously) in USA Pop Billboard Charts.
First to achieve the top six singles (simultaneously) in Australian Pop Charts.
First to have a million presales for a UK single (*I Want To Hold Your Hand*).
First to replace themselves at No 1 in the UK Charts (*I Want to Hold Your Hand* replacing *She Loves You* – 12th Dec 1963).

First to have two million presales for a US single (*Can't Buy Me Love*).
First English artist to break America.
First to own their own shop.
First to have entire album played on an English Radio station.
First to produce an album with no gaps between the tracks.
First to use wah-wah pedal.
First to have a fade-in single.
First to be awarded the MBE by their country.
First to have an EP in the singles charts.
First to have an album in the singles charts.
First to release a double EP.
First to have a double EP in the singles charts (and number 2 at that).
First to have twelve consecutive UK number one singles.
First to have eleven consecutive UK number one albums (all their official albums, in fact).

And first to split up!

And as all that was happening, The Beatles enjoyed a staggering 333 weeks on the UK singles charts. That's out of the possible 408 weeks from early 1963 to the end of the sixties. They spent 66 of those weeks languishing in the luxury of the coveted top spot. That 333 figure is a bit cosmic, isn't it? Not to mention one hell of an achievement. And if that wasn't enough, there's more. During the same period they were in the UK album top ten charts for 356 weeks in total. I mention the top ten here because in fairness hardly a week went by when The Beatles weren't somewhere in the charts (top 30) with an album or two. For 158 of the aforementioned 356 weeks in the top ten, The Beatles were number one. For a *further* 70 weeks they enjoyed the number two position. This was all before the split. Even after the break-up, Beatles albums were to continue to set sales records and enjoy chart placings that few could dream of touching.

The Beatles had achieved so much success already, even sacrificed part of their lives to do so. They were in a position where they didn't need to do it any more. Ever!

Lots of people, and a variety of circumstances, were blamed for the split. One of the more ludicrous suggestions was that they split because the rhythm guitarist's wife stole one of the lead guitarist's digestive biscuits. I mean, if it had been for a Jacobs Kimberley… but for a digestive, please!

Now, to me there are two predominant reasons why The Beatles disintegrated and subsequently split up between the making of *Sgt Pepper's* and the *White Album*. One, Brian Epstein died and, two, John Lennon met the person, Yoko Ono, for whom opportunism was an art form. Meeting her wasn't the decisive factor, though. Paul, George and Ringo were all in relationships at that time. But Jane, Patti and Maureen had not felt threatened by the closeness of the group, nor did they feel a need to destroy it. Yoko clung to John for her lifeblood. Everywhere John went, Yoko went, it was as simple and as awkward as that. And that included into the recording studio. For the first time one of them had introduced another person into the creative mix. And there were others as well, lawyers, would-be managers, general hangers-on, and I can tell you, the music business does produce its fair share of hangers-on.

Epstein's death was to affect the picture more than any of us could ever have predicted. He and The Beatles had worked hard, incredibly hard, over the years to set the operation up and, as it turns out, all they had created was a wealth beyond their wildest dreams. They had created an empire that a whole team of lawyers and accountants, all with their expensive metres running, were to going to fight over for the following twenty years.

I would suggest, respectfully, that if Brian Epstein had been around he would have discreetly dealt with the John *and* Yoko situation. I would also suggest that Brian would have put a team of people together to give the *Magical Mystery Tour* that extra bit of something it needed to make it brilliant. I mean, when you look at it today it looks great… nearly. Don't forget that although *A Hard Day's Night* looks like it was all very casual, unrehearsed and improvised, it was based on a very clever script by Alun Owen. One of the qualities Brian brought to the table was his ability to put together great people; the theatrical literary types he naturally liked to mix with. He was proud of this fact. *Magical Mystery Tour,* at least on paper, should have worked. And perhaps if the BBC had broadcast it in colour instead of black and white it would have received a different kind of attention. This was an oversight Brian Epstein would not have made.

Critically a bit of a meal was made over *The Magical Mystery Tour* special. It wasn't nearly as bad as the press proclaimed. It was just that this was the first time The Beatles had created something that was less than worthy of their genius, and the press who had been waiting in the wings, were sharpening their pencils. And how they vented their spleen as The Beatles showed for the first time that they might, after all, be mere mortals. To me though, critics are a bit like eunuchs; they sit around all day watching people do the wild thing knowing full well they'd never ever be able to do it themselves. All this frustration must cause some kind of resentment, don't you think?

Going back to Brian Epstein for a minute, I think he could have channelled the solo inclinations of John, Paul, George and Ringo and used them to the advantage of The Beatles rather than their detriment. Just small things, but important nonetheless, things like organising and co-ordinating the sabbaticals, re-grouping at a time to the band's creative and commercial advantage. Creatively, as I have mentioned, they needed to take a break from each other at the time they did. It was inevitable, of that there was no doubt. But my point here would have to be that had Brian Epstein been around, it would have been handled in a more discreet and friendly way, a way which would have allowed the boys to come back together, albeit several years later, to work on a project.

It had been mentioned many times that they, particularly John and Paul, had an ambition to create a musical. This would have been the perfect project to regroup for. Can you imagine how amazing that would have been? There are a few hints lurking around the body of their work for us to be able to hazard a guess. Like the opening of section of *Sgt Pepper's*, those first two songs were part of something greater. Add to that their flair for all things visual. Paul McCartney's *Eleanor Rigby*, *She's Leaving Home* and *Penny Lane*. All perfectly executed story-in-a-song approaches, so there is no doubt it could have been quite incredible. I'm sure Brian Epstein, with his theatrical flair and background, would have been over the moon if such a project had come into his sights.

More importantly, I feel that Brian Epstein would not have allowed the publishing situation (Dick James selling his shares of Northern Songs) to become the nightmare it did. Again, Mr Epstein would have contained the situation by buying back, for The Beatles, the shares Dick James wanted to unload. As it is, creative birthrights are currently being bought and sold around the world, as we speak, for obscene amounts of money. The most recent estimate is a staggering **one billion dollars!**

Personally, I would like to see a situation where one of this nation's genuine treasures (The Beatles' songs) are returned immediately to this country and to their rightful owners. I mean, imagine the fuss people would be making if we were talking about work on canvas or stone, rather than work on vinyl.

But in all of this, I'm not suggesting for one minute that Brian Epstein was a genius, for this was not the case. However, he really cared about The Beatles and to me this is the best quality a manager can process. Epstein would not have allowed them to split up. He did not look upon them as a meal ticket. He would have seen their growing wealth not as a bigger pie from which to cut a more generous portion for himself, but as something to look upon with a sense of pride. He'd have surely viewed it as something to use for the benefit of The Beatles and others. We've seen how each of The Beatles in later years did more than their fair share of benefits and charity work.

I'm absolutely positive that Brian would have brought the calm, and organisational skills, which Apple needed to turn it from a series of harebrained ideas into the true artists' co-operative The Beatles envisioned. Well as least as close to a co-operative as you could get when one party (The Beatles) were paying all the bills.

Far from having nothing to do now that 'his boys' had stopped touring, there was a multitude of things for Mr Epstein to get stuck into and get excited about. But no matter what, he would have continued to protect them. They were friends after all. There's one thing I felt touching at the time of his death. John, Paul, George and Ringo all talked about how devastated they were over losing a friend. With his death there were lots of parties whose prime interest was that the boys, who were once best of friends, would part as enemies. The old divide-and-conquer philosophy.

I know a lot of people will disagree with me, but I think The Beatles peaked with the albums *Rubber Soul* and *Revolver,* with *Sgt. Pepper's* completing the trilogy. Yes, after *Sgt Pepper's* they did make more music, and don't get me wrong, some very beautiful music at that. To me though it was not music they made as The Beatles, no, sadly more as four artists starting off on their solo careers. I'm talking here about the *White Album* of course.

Yellow Submarine was a great children's video and still is. The actors taking on Beatles accents launched the stage Liverpool accent on the world. *All Together Now*, a new track made for this project, was The Beatles being great at being The Beatles.

Let It Be on the other hand quite simply should never have been released. Giving us a free book didn't make up for a shoddy piece of work, particularly when we found out that someone interfered with the music (without the composers' permission) after the recording. A couple of good songs I suppose, yes of course, but they should have been released as part of the *Anthology* series. Then again, I don't really agree with all of that either. I do see the reason (anti-bootleggers) but perhaps there should have been a couple of great single albums in there somewhere, instead of three doubles.

Then again, if there had been a great single album, it would have come out at the time, wouldn't it? If you want to know the truth, if someone asked me to pick a best of The Beatles it would be easy, very easy. It would be *Please Please Me* as Volume One; *With The Beatles* would be Volume Two; *A Hard Day's Night* would be Volume Three; *Beatles For Sale* would be Volume Four; *Help!* would be Volume Five; *Rubber Soul* would be Volume Six; *Revolver* would be Volume Seven and Volume Eight would be *Sgt Pepper's Lonely Heart's Club Band*. Get the picture?

Only three Beatles turned up for their final recording session on Jan 3rd 1970. John Lennon was on holiday in Denmark. The final song they recorded was a George Harrison song called *I Me Mine*. Interesting that The Beatles' recording career should have been topped and tailed with George Harrison tunes.

They released one final single, *Let It Be* b/w *You Know My Name (Look Up The Number)* (Apple [Parlophone] R 5833, released on Friday 6th March 1970). Actually *they* didn't officially release any further records as The Beatles. At least one member that we know of (Paul) did not agree to re-mixing or adding strings or any of that stuff. But they were so busy with their own solo work at the time they didn't bother to try and stop the accountants putting together the *Let It Be* package. (Apple [Parlophone] Records PCS7096, released on 8th May 1970). Worth the money not for the freebie book but for the inclusion of *Across the Universe*, a 1968 recording, which now found a sad home as part of their swan song. I think they just didn't care about The Beatles any more and were happy enough to leave it to those who were pushing behind the scenes. Had things been different, perhaps that last single and album would never have been released.

But this isn't meant to be about their human flaws; this is meant to be about their greatness. The important thing is that The Beatles were bigger than all of that. They had reached the point of greatness that few, if any, ever achieve. They were in rare air, so rare in fact that no one, not even their best friends knew what it was like to be a Beatle; only four people ever enjoyed this state. That may seem like stating the obvious. The astronauts reached a similar state and apparently it's not always an altogether pleasant experience.

John, Paul, George, Ringo and the majority of their initial audience were the first generation to be born in the UK post World War Two. This generation was bonded together by the fact that they probably each had a father, or an older brother or uncle, who had been off fighting in the war. Even more like that they each had a relation who was one the three hundred thousand British fatalities in the war. The point is that each and every one of this generation knew someone who had either been wounded or killed in the war. As a reaction to all of this sadness and the pre-Second World War depression, there was a need to get out and enjoy, a need to be entertained. The Beatles' generation didn't cling to their family in the same way their parents had. They certainly enjoyed a lot more independence and freedom than their parents had. They were the first generation to have a disposable income. So they had money in their pockets, a thirst for life and itchy feet. The Beatles, with their vibrant joyous music, were the perfect means for this generation to let off steam. With their unique music, cool style, outspoken views, their need to explore all things musical and beyond, and their wacky humour, The Beatles provided the perfect soundtrack and backdrop for this era.

Initially that's *possibly* how or why The Beatles got started but it was *definitely* the quality of their songs and records that kept them going. The Beatles' music continues to sell on a worldwide scale unequalled by anyone before or since. Some reports suggest that their total worldwide career sales are either approaching the one billion mark or have just past it!

Even if it's only a fraction of that, it doesn't really matter; what really matters is the joy their music brought, and continues to bring, to the world.

And finally…

Sir Paul McCartney is still a Beatle.

Ringo Starr tours occasionally with The All Starrs and should be knighted immediately.

Sir George Martin has retired but still works for various charities.

Neil Aspinall quietly and effectively runs Apple.

Brian Epstein died on 23rd August 1967 from an accidental overdose of the drug carbitol.

Mal Evans, while behaving strangely, was shot four times and killed by the police in LA on 4th Jan 1976.

John Lennon was murdered on the street outside his New York home on 8th December 1980.

George Harrison sadly died after a long but dignified fight with cancer on 1st December 2001.

The Beatles Legacy:
5th Oct 1962 to 8th May 1970

For this section I have included only the UK releases, as I believe that's the way that God (and The Beatles) planned them to be released. EPs I have excluded for the most part as they were in effect re-packaging of singles and albums tracks.

THE SINGLES:

1: Love Me Do	P.S. I Love You
2: Please Please Me	Ask Me Why
3: From Me To You	Thank You Girl
4: She Loves You	I'll Get You
5: I Want To Hold Your Hand	This Boy
6: Can't Buy Me Love	You Can't Do That
7: A Hard Day's Night	Things We Said Today
8: I Feel Fine	She's A Woman
9: Ticket To Ride	Yes It Is
10: Help!	I'm Down
11: We Can Work It Out	Day Tripper
12: Paperback Writer	Rain
13: Eleanor Rigby	Yellow Submarine
14: Strawberry Fields Forever	Penny Lane
15: All You Need Is Love	Baby You're a Rich Man
16: Hello Goodbye	I Am The Walrus
17: Lady Madonna	The Inner Light
18: Hey Jude	Revolution
19: Get Back	Don't Let Me Down
20: The Ballad of John & Yoko	Old Brown Shoe
21: Something	Come Together
22: Let It Be	You Know My Name (Look Up The Number)

THE ALBUMS:

1: *Please Please Me*:

I Saw Her Standing There
Misery
Anna (Go To Him)
Chains
Boys
Ask Me Why
Please Please Me

Love Me Do
P.S. I Love You
Baby It's You
Do You Want To Know a Secret
A Taste of Honey
There's A Place
Twist and Shout

2: *With The Beatles*:

It Won't Be Long
All I've Got To Do
All My Loving
Don't Bother Me
Little Child
Till There Was You
Please Mr Postman

Roll Over Beethoven
Hold Me Tight
You Really Got A Hold On Me
I Wanna Be Your Man
Devil In Her Heart
Not a Second Time
Money (That's What I Want)

3: *A Hard Day's Night*:

A Hard Day's Night
I Should Have Known Better
If I Fell
I'm Happy Just To Dance
And I Love Her
Tell Me Why
Can't Buy Me Love

Any Time At All
I'll Cry Instead
Things We Said Today
When I Get Home
You Can't Do That
I'll Be Back

4: *Beatles For Sale*:

No Reply
I'm A Loser
Baby's In Black
Rock and Roll Music
I'll Follow The Sun
Mr. Moonlight
Kansas City

Eight Days A Week
Words Of Love
Honey Don't
Every Little Thing
I Don't Want To Spoil The Party
What You're Doing
Everybody's Trying To Be My
   Baby

5: *Help!*:

Help!	Act Naturally
The Night Before	It's Only Love
You've Got To Hide Your Love	You Like Me Too Much
I Need You	Tell Me What You See
Another Girl	I've Just Seen a Face
You're Going To Lose That Girl	Yesterday
Ticket To Ride	Dizzy Miss Lizzy

6: *Rubber Soul:*

Drive My Car	What Goes On
Norwegian Wood	Girl
You Won't See Me	I'm Looking Thro You
Nowhere Man	In My Life
Think For Yourself	Wait
The Word	If I Needed Someone
Michelle	Run For Your Life

7: *Revolver*:

Taxman	Good Day Sunshine
Eleanor Rigby	And Your Bird Can Sing
I'm Only Sleeping	For No One
Love You To	Doctor Robert
Here, There and EverywhereI	Want To Tell You
Yellow Submarine	Got To Get You Into My Life
She Said She Said	Tomorrow Never Knows

8: *Sgt Pepper's Lonely Hearts Club Band*:

Sgt Pepper's Lonely Hearts Club Band	Within You Without You
With A Little Help From My Friends	When I'm Sixty-Four
Lucy in The Sky With Diamonds	Lovely Rita
Getting Better	Good Morning Good Morning
Fixing a Hole	Sgt Pepper's Lonely Heart's Club Band (Reprise)
She's Leaving Home	
Being For The Benefit Of Mr Kite	A Day in The Life

9: *The Beatles*:

Back In The USSR

Dear Prudence

Glass Onion

Ob-La-Di, Ob-La-Da

Wild Honey Pie

The Continuing Story Of
   Bungalow Bill

While My Guitar
Gently Weeps

Happiness is a Warm Gun

Martha My Dear

I'm So Tired

Blackbird

Piggies

Rocky Raccoon

Don't Pass Me By

Why Don't We Do It In The Road

I Will

Julia

Birthday

Yer Blues

Mother Nature's Sun

Everybody's Got Something
   To Hide Except For Me
   And My Monkey

Sexy Sadie

Helter Skelter

Long Long Long

Revolution 1

Honey Pie

Savoy Truffle

Cry Baby Cry

Revolution 9

Goodnight

10: *Abbey Road*:

Come Together

Something

Maxwell's Silver Hammer

Oh Darling

Octupus's Garden

I Want You (She's So Heavy)

Here Comes The Sun

Because

You Never Give Me Your Money

Sun King

Mean Mr. Mustard

Polythene Pam

She Came in Through The
   Bathroom Window

Golden Slumbers

Carry That Weight

The End

Her Majesty

11: *Let It Be*:

Two Of Us

Dig A Pony

Across The Universe

I Me Mine

Dig It

Let It Be

Maggie May

I've Got A Feeling

The One After 909

The Long and Winding Road

For You Blue

Get Back

BEATLES SONGS ON
YELLOW SUBMARINE SOUNDTRACK ALBUM:

Only A Northern Song

Hey Bulldog

All Together Now

It's All Too Much.

DOUBLE EP:

Magical Mystery Tour:

Magical Mystery Tour

Your Mother Should Know

I Am The Walrus

The Fool On The Hill

Flying

Blue Jay Way.

TRACKS NOT INCLUDED ON ANY OF THE ABOVE

Bad Boy (A Collection of Oldies... But Goldies LP)

Matchbox (from Long Tall Sally EP)

RECOMMENDED ASSOCIATED ALBUMS:

All Things Must Pass.	George Harrison
Wilburys Vol 1.	The Travelling Wilburys
Imagine	John Lennon
Band On The Run	Wings
Ringo	Ringo Starr

RECOMMENDED FILMS:

A Hard Day's Night	The Beatles
Help!	The Beatles
Let It Be	The Beatles
Backbeat	
The Hours and Times	

RECOMMENDED VIDEOS.

The Anthology Series	The Beatles
Magical Mystery Tour	The Beatles
The Beatles At Shea Stadium	The Beatles

VITAL READING

The Beatles Anthology	The Beatles

RECOMMENDED BOOKS:

I Me Mine	George Harrison
The Summer of Love - The Making Of Sgt Pepper's	George Martin
A Cellar Full of Noise	Brian Epstein
Fifty Years Adrift	Derek Taylor
It Was Twenty Years Ago Today	Derek Taylor
The Complete Beatles Chronicle	Mark Lewisohn
The Complete Beatles Recording Sessions	Mark Lewisohn
The Ultimate Beatle Encyclopedia	Bill Harry.
Yesterday & Today	Ray Coleman
Evolution of The Beatles 1957-1970	Pete Frame
First of the True Believers	Paul Charles

The Essential Library: Recent Music Releases

Build up your library with new titles every month

How To Succeed In The Music Business by Paul Charles

As an agent, a manager and a promoter for some of the biggest names in the business since 1975, Paul Charles has all the information you need to make a start in the music business either as an artist or on the business side.

Whether you're an aspiring singer songwriter or want to form a group with a bunch of your friends and you need to know how to launch your career. The music business can appear quite daunting with all it's apparently cool people, buzzwords and in-phrases, but the reality is that it's very simple. This book discusses the various professionals you'll come into contact with and what exactly they should be doing for you.

The Beastie Boys by Richard Luck

From swilling beer and swiping VW-badges to universal respect and hanging out with the Dalai Lama, no one has taken a musical journey to rival that of The Beastie Boys. Their journey from fighting for their right to party to campaigning to free Tibet, encompasses tabloid notoriety, terrible films, terrific videos and trailblazing hip-hop. The founders of the Grand Royal empire, the architects of Nu Metal and proof positive that white guys really can rap.

Jethro Tull by Raymond Benson

Jethro Tull formed in 1968 and is still going strong, thanks to the leadership, vision and extraordinary talent of its leader, Ian Anderson. Anderson's band has always been controversial, challenging and completely impossible to categorise. Are they rock? Blues? Progressive? English folk? These labels merely begin to describe Jethro Tull's eclectic and imaginative music. In the thirty-five years of the band's existence, Tull's music has gone through many styles and periods, just as the group has undergone several personnel changes. Nevertheless, the band has always produced distinctive 'Tull Music.'

The Madchester Scene by Richard Luck

The home of legendary acts such as New Order and The Smiths, the early 1990s saw Manchester give birth to great groups like the Happy Mondays, James and The Stone Roses. Blending the attitudes of The Fall and the Buzzcocks with cutting edge sampling techniques and the occasional chemical, these bands created the superb 'Madchester' sound. *The Madchester Scene* profiles all the major bands, together with the groups that influenced them and the swines that ripped them off.

The Essential Library: History Best-Sellers

Build up your library with new titles published every month

Conspiracy Theories by Robin Ramsay

Do you think *The X-Files* is fiction? That Elvis is dead? That the US actually went to the moon? And don't know that the ruling elite did a deal with the extra-terrestrials after the Roswell crash in 1947... At one time, you could blame the world's troubles on the Masons or the Illuminati, or the Jews, or One Worlders, or the Great Communist Conspiracy. Now we also have the alien-US elite conspiracy, or the alien shape-shifting reptile conspiracy to worry about - and there are books to prove it as well! This book tries to sort out the handful of wheat from the choking clouds of intellectual chaff. For among the nonsensical Conspiracy Theory rubbish currently proliferating on the Internet, there are important nuggets of real research about real conspiracies waiting to be mined.

The Rise Of New Labour by Robin Ramsay

The rise of New Labour? How did that happen? As everybody knows, Labour messed up the economy in the 1970s, went too far to the left, became 'unelectable' and let Mrs Thatcher in. After three General Election defeats Labour modernised, abandoned the left and had successive landslide victories in 1997 and 2001.

That's the story they print in newspapers. The only problem is...the real story of the rise of New Labour is more complex, and it involves the British and American intelligence services, the Israelis and elite management groups like the Bilderbergers.

Robin Ramsay untangles the myths and shows how it really happened that Gordon Brown sank gratefully into the arms of the bankers, Labour took on board the agenda of the City of London, and that nice Mr Blair embraced his role as the last dribble of Thatcherism down the leg of British politics.

UFOs by Neil Nixon

UFOs and Aliens have been reported throughout recorded time. Reports of UFO incidents vary from lights in the sky to abductions. The details are frequently terrifying, always baffling and occasionally hilarious. This book includes the best known cases, the most incredible stories and the answers that explain them. There are astounding and cautionary tales which suggest that the answers we seek may be found in the least likely places.

The Essential Library: Film Best-Sellers

Build up your library with new titles every month

Film Noir by Paul Duncan

The laconic private eye, the corrupt cop, the heist that goes wrong, the femme fatale with the rich husband and the dim lover - these are the trademark characters of Film Noir. This book charts the progression of the Noir style as a vehicle for film-makers who wanted to record the darkness at the heart of American society as it emerged from World War to the Cold War. As well as an introduction explaining the origins of Film Noir, seven films are examined in detail and an exhaustive list of over 500 Films Noirs are listed.

Alfred Hitchcock by Paul Duncan

More than 20 years after his death, Alfred Hitchcock is still a household name, most people in the Western world have seen at least one of his films, and he popularised the action movie format we see every week on the cinema screen. He was both a great artist and dynamite at the box office. This book examines the genius and enduring popularity of one of the most influential figures in the history of the cinema!

Orson Welles by Martin Fitzgerald

The popular myth is that after the artistic success of *Citizen Kane* it all went downhill for Orson Welles, that he was some kind of fallen genius. Yet, despite overwhelming odds, he went on to make great Films Noirs like *The Lady From Shanghai* and *Touch Of Evil*. He translated Shakespeare's work into films with heart and soul (*Othello*, *Chimes At Midnight*, *Macbeth*), and he gave voice to bitterness, regret and desperation in *The Magnificent Ambersons* and *The Trial*. Far from being down and out, Welles became one of the first cutting-edge independent film-makers.

Stanley Kubrick by Paul Duncan

Kubrick's work, like all masterpieces, has a timeless quality. His vision is so complete, the detail so meticulous, that you believe you are in a three-dimensional space displayed on a two-dimensional screen. He was commercially successful because he embraced traditional genres like War (*Paths Of Glory*, *Full Metal Jacket*), Crime (*The Killing*), Science Fiction (*2001*), Horror (*The Shining*) and Love (*Barry Lyndon*). At the same time, he stretched the boundaries of film with controversial themes: underage sex (*Lolita*); ultra violence (*A Clockwork Orange*); and erotica (*Eyes Wide Shut*).

The Essential Library: Currently Available

Film Directors:

Woody Allen (2nd)	Tim Burton	Ang Lee
Jane Campion*	John Carpenter	Joel & Ethan Coen (2nd)
Jackie Chan	Steven Soderbergh	Clint Eastwood
David Cronenberg	Terry Gilliam*	Michael Mann
Alfred Hitchcock (2nd)	Krzysztof Kieslowski*	Roman Polanski
Stanley Kubrick (2nd)	Sergio Leone	Oliver Stone
David Lynch (2nd)	Brian De Palma*	George Lucas
Sam Peckinpah*	Ridley Scott (2nd)	James Cameron
Orson Welles (2nd)	Billy Wilder	Roger Corman
Steven Spielberg	Mike Hodges	Spike Lee

Film Genres:

Blaxploitation Films	Bollywood	French New Wave
Horror Films	Spaghetti Westerns	Vietnam War Movies
Slasher Movies	Film Noir	Hammer Films
Vampire Films*	Heroic Bloodshed*	Carry On Films
German Expressionist Films		

Film Subjects:

Laurel & Hardy	Marx Brothers	Film Music
Steve McQueen*	Marilyn Monroe	The Oscars® (2nd)
Filming On A Microbudget	Bruce Lee	Writing A Screenplay
Film Studies		

Music:

The Madchester Scene	Beastie Boys	Jethro Tull
How To Succeed In The Music Business		The Beatles

Literature:

Cyberpunk	Philip K Dick	The Beat Generation
Agatha Christie	Sherlock Holmes	Noir Fiction
Terry Pratchett	Hitchhiker's Guide (2nd)	Alan Moore
William Shakespeare	Creative Writing	Tintin
Georges Simenon		

Ideas:

Conspiracy Theories	Nietzsche	UFOs
Feminism	Freud & Psychoanalysis	Bisexuality

History:

Alchemy & Alchemists	The Crusades	The Black Death
Jack The Ripper	The Rise Of New Labour	Ancient Greece
American Civil War	American Indian Wars	Witchcraft
Globalisation	Who Shot JFK?	

Miscellaneous:

Stock Market Essentials	How To Succeed As A Sports Agent	Doctor Who

Available at bookstores or send a cheque (payable to 'Oldcastle Books') to: **Pocket Essentials (Dept BT)**, P O Box 394, Harpenden, Herts, AL5 1XJ, UK. £3.99 each (£2.99 if marked with an *). For each book add 50p(UK)/£1 (elsewhere) postage & packing